VISION FOR A CHRISTIAN COLLEGE

Essays by
Gordon J. Van Wylen

The Historical Series of the Reformed Church in America
No. 18

VISION
FOR A
CHRISTIAN COLLEGE

Essays by
Gordon J. Van Wylen
President of Hope College, 1972-87

Edited by Harry Boonstra

WM. B. EERDMANS PUBLISHING COMPANY
GRAND RAPIDS, MICHIGAN

Copyright © 1988 Wm. B. Eerdmans Publishing Company
255 Jefferson S.E. Grand Rapids, Michigan 49503

Library of Congress Cataloging-in-Publication Data

Van Wylen, Gordon John.
    Vision for a Christian college: essays / by Gordon J. Van Wylen;
edited by Harry Boonstra.
        p.   cm.   (The Historical series of the Reformed Church in
America; no. 18)
    ISBN 0-8028-0441-1
    1. Hope College—History. 2. Church colleges—Michigan—Holland—
History. 3. Education, Higher—Philosophy. I. Boonstra, Harry.
II. Title. III. Series.
LD2281.H62V36 1988
378.774'15—dc19   88-25928
                                                                    CIP

To
The Hope College Family
with gratitude
for fifteen years of fellowship and service
in the gracious, purposeful academic community
God entrusted to us

The Historical Series of the Reformed Church in America

This series has been inaugurated by the General Synod of the Reformed Church in America, acting through its Commission on History, for the purpose of encouraging historical research and providing a medium wherein this knowledge may be shared with the academic community and with the members of the denomination in order that a knowledge of the past may contribute to right action in the present.

General Editor
The Rev. Donald J. Bruggink, Ph.D., Western Theological Seminary

Commission on History
The Rev. Benjamin Alicea, New Brunswick Theological Seminary
Bette L. Brunsting, M.A., Central College
Professor Gerald F. DeJong, Ph.D., University of South Dakota
Glenna Foster, Union City, California
Professor Earl Wm. Kennedy, Th.D., Northwestern College
The Rev. Edwin G. Mulder, D.D., General Secretary,
    Reformed Church in America
The Rev. Dennis Voskuil, Ph.D., Hope College

Recognitions

Mr. Peter Huizenga, a member of the Board of Trustees, first envisioned this collection of essays. We are grateful to him for this vision and for his generous financial support. We thank Elton J. Bruins, Evert J. and Hattie E. Blekkink Professor of Religion at Hope College, for his constant encouragement of the project and for co-authoring the introductory essay. Ms. Ann W. Farley, administrative assistant to the dean for Arts and Humanities, and Ms. Judy A. Brake, administrative assistant in the Business Office, provided invaluable word processing assistance. The late Ms. Charlotte A. Mulder, administrative assistant to President Van Wylen, provided constant help in gaining access to documents in the President's office.

H. B.

Contents

Preface

President Van Wylen did extensive writing during his fifteen years at Hope College. Of course, much of this writing consisted of routine reports and papers common to any large organization today. But a substantial part of the writing went beyond the routine presidential memo and thank you letter. A significant segment contained Van Wylen's vision for Hope College and for Christian education generally.

The occasions for such writing were many and diverse. A large number of the essays were presented as addresses at the beginning of each school year. The faculty and staff have typically begun the year with a (off campus or on campus) "retreat," which has always included an opening address by the president. There would be the usual nuts and bolts information for the new year, such as enrollment figures and the welcome of new faculty. But most years a substantial section of the talk was devoted to a fundamental aspect of college life or of Christian higher education. Other occasions might be a memo sharing that vision with college supporters, or a letter explaining the purpose of Hope College to state officials. In addition, the president regularly spoke in the College chapel, preached in many churches, shared his insight with InterVarsity groups, and wrote magazine articles.

When reviewing the wide array of materials, the selection committee decided to focus on President Van Wylen's educational writings. Although his devotional pieces, chapel talks, or high school commencement addresses were worth sharing with a wider audience, these did not directly relate to his principal task of leading Hope College. We therefore decided to select only those essays which deal with educational issues, especially those which embody his vision of combining faith and learning and the practical implementation of such a vision.

Nearly all of these essays were first presented as lectures,

talks, and addresses. In editing them I have been mindful that
they will now be perused as written documents, but have tried to
maintain some of the flavor of the oral presentations. Nearly all
of the essays have been shortened, usually by deleting that which
seems ephemeral for a longer perspective.

The genesis and the audience of these essays were mostly at
Hope College, and the collection will have special appeal to current, past, and future faculty, students, boards, and supporters of
the College and the Reformed Church in America. The collection
constitutes a mini-history of fifteen years in the life of Hope College.

But the essays are not narrowly parochial. What Van Wylen
says about and for Hope College is often applicable to other colleges, especially Christian colleges. Questions of academic freedom, honor codes, minority students, financial solvency, and
particularly the purpose and mission of Christian colleges go beyond Hope College and Holland, Michigan. We therefore trust
that others interested in Christian higher education will want to
look over the College's shoulders—not so much to see a model
college, as to observe a case history. Here is a school which takes
its Christian heritage seriously and which tries to understand and
serve the world in which we live. May this collection of a president's and a college's vision inspire others, in their contexts, to
work out this same vision.

HARRY BOONSTRA
Editor

Gordon J. Van Wylen
and Hope College

Gordon Van Wylen came to Hope College in 1972 and left the presidency upon his retirement in 1987. What impact did he have on Hope College? What achievements was he responsible for? What direction did the college take under his leadership? Such questions cannot be answered fully so soon after his tenure; a future historian of Hope College will have to make such assessments. But we can, at this time, provide a more short-range description of Van Wylen's presidency, an interim report of his years at Hope. We provide such a description by sketching both the history of Hope College to 1972 and the nature of Hope College as a Christian college, and then suggesting briefly how President Van Wylen helped to shape Hope College. The emphasis in this essay will be especially on Hope College as an institution of Christian higher education.

I.
HISTORICAL SKETCH OF HOPE COLLEGE

The beginning of Hope College is inextricably linked with the establishment of the Dutch immigrant churches in the Midwest. When Dominie Albertus van Raalte and his small group of followers settled in the wilds of western Michigan in 1847, they were motivated by a number of considerations. Certainly economic security was one of those, but the search for religious security was even more important. They were a part of the 1834 Secession from The Netherlands Reformed Church and had experienced harassment from both ecclesiastical and civic authorities. They longed for a church in which they could practice their deep pietism and their fidelity to the Reformed confessions, and they wanted the freedom to establish their own schools. On these points there was unanimity among the settlers.

But there were also profound differences in the community. Some of these were doctrinal and ecclesiastical, but the differences were especially sharp in their views of education. Most of Van Raalte's followers were people with very little schooling or cultural exposure and even his fellow ministers had received limited education. Van Raalte, on the other hand, had received a university education (Leiden) and moved easily in academic and cultural circles. These educational and cultural differences were to surface frequently in the early years of Hope College.

The disagreements came to expression especially as the colony struggled to establish a school. The people seemed to have been open to the idea of the Pioneer School (later the Holland Academy), which was begun in 1851 and formally adopted by the General Synod of the RCA in 1857. But when the Academy was incorporated as a college in 1866 the support became less substantial. The immigrants appeared to see the need for primary instruction (and, as we shall see presently, ministerial education), but were much less inclined to support the secondary and college levels. Van Raalte, however, championed the cause of education at all levels and insisted on a thorough classical training; he even supported President Philip Phelps's (the first president) misguided dream of expanding the fledgling college to a university.

The question about the purpose of education came to very pointed expression in the controversy over the teaching of theology. The immigrants, who had become a part of the old "Dutch Reformed Church" (now the Reformed Church in America), were committed to education if the school would give Christian instruction to their young children and would provide them with ministers. However, since the RCA already had New Brunswick Seminary in the East, the General Synod (which was funding the College) was not kindly disposed to offering ministerial training at Hope College. But the western churches prevailed and a

"Theological School at Hope College" was added in 1866. However, financial difficulties forced the General Synod to close the theological department in 1877. The people of Holland were not pleased! The Holland *City News* was not averse to biting the hand that fed the College: "We have yet to hear one good reason from the rich descendants of our forefathers in the East. Why will they not put their hands in their pockets and help the institution . . . ?"[1]

The General Synod was not swayed by this and other pleading from the West and the theology department was not restored at that time. But the West was not to be denied. They renewed their pleas for theological education as essential for the life of the church. (They also argued their case by suggesting a wholesome influence for the college: "Return to our college boys the blessing of the godly example of their more advanced brethren."[2]) In 1884, General Synod, perhaps to test the commitment of the western church, agreed to a restoration, but only if the West would raise sufficient funds to endow a chair of theology. The West promptly raised $30,000—a formidable amount for the immigrant churches. But this success also meant the separation of the theological department from Hope College. Synod decided that the ministerial training could be best performed if it were in a separate institution, and therefore established Western Theological Seminary.

The issue of financial support was probably a good barometer of the West's commitment to Hope College. Both the pietistic leanings and the limited education of most of the immigrants made them value ministerial training over general education. The West raised $30,000 for theological education in 1884, but in 1910 total church contributions to Hope College amounted to only $151.

Indeed, the overwhelming impression one receives when reading the history of Hope College is that the College was, to a great degree, the creation of Van Raalte and the eastern church. Van

Raalte was untiring in his promotion of the Academy and the College and spent untold days and miles raising support in the East. And the eastern churches, especially a number of wealthy individuals, contributed very generously. The liberality was probably prompted by a combination of genuine love for the immigrant church and by Van Raalte's "importunate widow" persistence. (However, at times "some of the early benefactors of the college were beginning to question the financial acumen of a Council composed almost entirely of ministers."[3]) Overall, the fund-raising results were impressive. For example, Provisional President G. Henry Mandeville raised $20,000 in New York City between 1878 and 1882, Garrett Kouwenhoven of Long Island donated $13,000 in 1881, and in 1893 Nathan F. Graves of Syracuse, New York, donated $10,000 for a new library. Of course, one has to remember that the western churches consisted largely of immigrants scratching out a precarious existence, while the eastern churches had many families with accumulated wealth and extensive business holdings. Still, one cannot escape the impression that the East had more heart for the development of Hope College than did the West.[4]

But even though Hope College was, in some ways, more a college of the East than of its immediate constituency, and even though the financial resources were not always forthcoming, it was, in other ways, a true college of the whole church. There was never any doubt that Hope College "belonged to" the RCA. All the presidents and professors (until the 1940s) were members of the RCA, as were the members of the Council or Board of Trustees. The members of the board were appointed by synod and classis and (until 1967) were predominantly clergy.

Since the 1960s there have been a number of changes in the relationship between Hope College and the RCA. The legal "ownership" of the college passed from the General Synod to the Board of Trustees in 1960, and in 1967 the board structure was changed. Instead of an all-clergy board, there now were six clergy and six laypersons appointed by General Synod, in addition to a maximum of nineteen other members at large, not necessarily from the RCA. Hope College is no longer a college "of the RCA," but "affiliated with the RCA."

So far we have traced the history of Hope College largely as it was related to the RCA—especially in terms of financial support and governing structure. But one can survey its history also by shifting the focus to areas such as the nature of the College, the composition of the faculty, the students and their life-styles.

As suggested above, the immigrant churches often looked upon Hope College primarily as an institution to train ministers; and certainly the College fulfilled that role admirably, first by providing clergy with their full theological training, later by providing students with an appropriate pre-seminary training. Hope has an illustrious array of clergy graduates who served in parishes, mission fields, and classrooms.

But the purpose of the College was always wider than ministerial training. The early curriculum included courses in the classics, and around the turn of the century the College introduced courses in the sciences and in education. The humanities were represented in the English and foreign language courses, and Hope approved a bachelor of music program in the 1920s. Since then the College has expanded to a full-fledged curriculum of some twenty-five majors, with research activities in all disciplines and performances in the arts.

Given this broadening of the curriculum, how did Hope seek to maintain its Christian heritage? How did the College keep from going the route of many other American colleges which lost their Christian heritage when they broadened into "secular" areas? First, there was the recognition that service in God's church and kingdom is not limited to ministerial roles. All professions lend themselves to service of humanity, and the College sought to instill a sense of service in its graduates, no matter what their vocational orientation. The College also attempted to maintain a Christian focus in its curriculum. Courses in biblical studies and theology (from a Reformed perspective) were required of all students, and the orientation in the curriculum honored the Christian tradition. Another area of concern was the general spiritual tone of the College. Chapel attendance was required until 1970, and students were encouraged to be involved in prayer groups, Bible studies, and service projects.

Hope further sought to maintain a Christian posture in its selection of faculty. In its early years all faculty were members of the RCA, but after World War I professors from other evangelical Protestant traditions began to join the faculty. During the 1960s the religious affiliation of the faculty became much wider, including Roman Catholic and Orthodox, and a number of faculty had no religious affiliation, while others did not support the College's Christian tradition. Thus the earlier theological cohesion was weakened and the Christian mission of the college became more diffuse.

In terms of admitting students, Hope College had always been more open than most other Christian colleges; the College never attempted to define its religious nature by admitting only Christian students, and the student body of the College has always been religiously diverse. The 1865 "Articles of Incorporation" specified: "Although the College is denominational in character, yet students shall be admitted to all its advantages, without respect to their ecclesiastical connections, subject only to the general rules and regulations of the Institution." And, unlike many other Christian colleges, Hope never required a testimony of faith from its entering students. Still, during the first half of its history most of the students were members of the RCA.

One interesting aspect about the RCA students was their reason for attending Hope. When reading the history of the College in terms of student behavior and in the pages of the student newspaper, *The Anchor,* it becomes obvious that for many students the

College became a release from a very conservative home and church life. Many students saw Hope College as a way to express their independence, or to escape from the confines of Dutch-American provincialism. Of course, the College officials and the Board of Trustees were not always willing to grant much independence. The code of behavior was circumscribed, and social activities were severely restricted. Sports were initially frowned on, and the students had to engage in extensive lobbying and a student strike before they were granted permission to engage in intercollegiate sports in 1914. Drama was not permitted until a student club began its first productions in 1939, and dances on campus were not allowed until the early 1950s. These strictures were not unusual for Christian colleges, but they do demonstrate the presence of a conservative constituency and the increasing diversity of the College.

II.
WHAT KIND OF CHRISTIAN COLLEGE IS HOPE COLLEGE?

There are hundreds of American colleges which have been classified as "Christian" colleges. Two common ways of categorizing Christian colleges are, first, in terms of a college's relationship to a denomination, and secondly, how the Christian faith makes an impact on the life of the college. We will briefly survey Hope College along the same lines.

One model for distinguishing Christian academic institutions in terms of denominational affiliation was suggested by Hobbs and Meeth in *Diversity Among Christian Colleges.*[5] They distinguish four types of relationships to a denomination: a) the historically denominational college, b) the denomination-related college, c) the college-of-the-denomination, and d) the non-denominational college.

In its relationship to the Reformed Church in America Hope College probably has its feet in both b) and c), or it may be more correct to say that Hope has traveled from c) to b). A college-of-the-denomination has very strong structural ties with a denomination, is often governed by the denomination's judicial body, and "deliberately and systematically seeks to educate the denomination's members."[6] The denominationally related college has less prominent ties. Instead of being a college of the church, it is "affiliated with" a church, usually with "a statement of faith which is consonant with the distinctive doctrines of the denomination"[7], and the board of trustees usually includes a given number of representatives from the denomination. Twenty-five years ago Hope College would probably have been classified as a college-of-the denomination, but today it is rightly seen as a denominationally related college; it officially designates itself as "affiliated with" the RCA.

Merrimon Cuninggim[8] provides another model for describing Christian colleges, when he delineates: a) the consonant college (the ally); b) the proclaiming college (the witness); and c) the embodying college (the reflection). Today Hope College is certainly not an embodying college, that is, it is not a mirror of the RCA. At certain times Hope may act like a proclaiming college—"an institution that joyously announces its affiliation with its sponsoring denomination at every appropriate occasion."[9] This category does not suggest that a college usurps the role of the church, or neglects its main task. Rather, "The Proclaiming College is the acknowledged academic partner of the church, taking seriously both its intellectual and its ecclesiastical character."[10]

But in most aspects Hope can be better designated as an ally, a consonant college. Cuninggim's definition nicely captures Hope College:

> The Consonant College is an institution that, feeling independent in its own operations, is committed to the tradition of its related church and to consistency with that tradition in its

own behavior. Its values are in the main its denomination's values. They are taken seriously and are evident in the life of the college and the lives of its alumni/ae.[11]

Hope College certainly is not a college that is "run by" the church; it is independent in its governing structure and in setting its course. But the College does take the tradition of the RCA seriously, in that it seeks to steer its way in the stream of "the historic Christian faith," and at times more narrowly in the Reformed tradition. And even though the values and life-styles among faculty and students show a wider spectrum than one would typically find among RCA constituency, the College does espouse the values resident in the RCA. As Cuninggim says of another consonant college: It "understands itself to be free from the church as well as from the state, and this status frees it not to be either secular or sectarian but to be seriously concerned with religious study and worship in ways harmonious with its . . . heritage and present relationship."[12]

There are, obviously, other ways of characterizing the relationship between Hope College and the RCA, but "denominationally related," or "consonant college" are helpful ways of designating the relationship between school and church. The "Covenant of Mutual Responsibilities" drawn up between the RCA and Hope College (and Central and Northwestern colleges) summarizes well the spirit suggested by a "consonant" college relationship. The covenant speaks of a strong commitment to the Christian heritage and "maintaining a friendly appreciation for the Reformed tradition and its implications for faith and learning." The RCA, in turn, pledges its encouragement and support for the colleges.

Another way of designating Christian colleges is in terms of the impact of the Christian faith on the life of the college. Or, put more explicitly, what decisions does a college make on how and where the faith impinges on the governmental, academic, social, and spiritual life of the college, and what are the implications of such decisions on board composition or faculty hiring or the mix of students or student behavior? Here one is often hard-pressed to delineate a college's stance clearly, since one deals with many facets of the institution, some of which may be at odds with the college's main tenets, and one often finds a college in a state of flux. But again, we will try to sketch the broad outlines.

Here we will use categories suggested by William C. Ringenberg in his *The Christian College.*[13] Ringenberg's study is weighted somewhat toward fundamentalist and evangelical schools, but it does in many ways "fit" Hope College. After reviewing the history of Christian colleges, Ringenberg briefly describes "The Emerging Identity of the Modern Christian College."[14] He outlines five characteristics of the modern Christian college:

1) a growing quality

2) an enlarged intellectual openness within the realm of orthodoxy

3) an increasing effort to integrate faith, learning, and living

4) a continuing effort to promote spiritual nurture and character development

5) an increased degree of intercollegiate cooperation.

How does Hope College fare in those categories?

1. "Quality" is a slippery term which can be read very subjectively. Nevertheless, an impartial observer of Hope College would certainly admit that the College has gained in quality in many areas. The most visible improvement during the past two decades has been in the College campus. New buildings have been added, old buildings beautifully renovated, educational equipment greatly improved, all enhanced by a fine overall campus appearance. Less visible but more important has been the solidification of the academic program. Hope's stature in scientific research and education has been well-attested during the past

twenty years, as the College has acquired an enviable national reputation. But other disciplines in the College have also made significant contributions. Whether one measures such achievement in faculty publications or student admissions to graduate and professional schools or career and service accomplishments of graduates—the academic growth of the College has been substantial. Similarly, achievements in the arts, as attested in exhibits, concerts, and performances, have made a significant mark.

2. With the phrase "enlarged intellectual openness within the realm of orthodoxy" Ringenberg wants to suggest academic exploration within certain limits. Since part of his book laments inroads of secularism into erstwhile Christian colleges, he does not advise unlimited intellectual openness, but wants the intellectual search infused with and circumscribed by biblical teaching. The "orthodoxy" held to by Hope College has during the past two decades been defined as "the historic Christian faith," and in a number of intense discussions the college has attempted to "unpack" that phrase. A study paper written by Marc Baer, Kenneth Elzinga, and Dennis Voskuil (included in Gordon Van Wylen's "What We Owe Our Institutional Heirs," 1985) addresses this issue as follows:

> We align ourselves with the central affirmations of the Christian church which were rooted in the Bible and given shape during the Apostolic era. The term "historic" links us directly to our Reformation forebears who sought to reaffirm the central tenets of the New Testament Church. And while it recalls our specific Dutch Reformed heritage, it also suggests inclusiveness based on a common core of religious convictions.[15]

The openness of the College has probably gone beyond that envisioned for evangelical colleges by Ringenberg, since Hope College includes faculty from Roman Catholic and Orthodox background.

3. An "increasing effort to integrate faith, learning, and living"

does characterize Hope College. Again, the Baer, et al., paper discusses various components of this integration, including faculty recruitment, the presence of non-Christian students, and the imparting of this integration in the classroom. Hope College provides its students with a perspective in which Christian values govern class discussions and provide "the foundations for human morality and ethics; it rests upon the conviction that there are ultimate standards for justice, equity, and truth."[16] The degree to which various faculty are involved in this integration of the Christian faith and learning varies enormously at Hope College, depending both on the field of study and on the conviction, experience, and theological perspectives of the faculty members.

4. At Hope College "spiritual nurture and character development" take many different forms. Certainly the work of the chaplain's office takes a major role here. The worship services during the week and on Sunday mornings are the most visible ways of nurturing the students spiritually. The other ministry dimensions of the chaplain's office, such as counseling or promoting leadership, are shared by others on campus, including the Counseling Center and many faculty. In addition, most of Hope faculty and staff are conscious of their modeling role for students and therefore lead mature Christian lives. But Hope College is also aware that the nurturing of students is not accomplished best by trying to cast students in the same mold. There is a strong awareness that students have to develop their own values and life-styles; and even though the College wishes to have these values infused with the Christian faith, it is also important that students become independent in their choices and decisions. Thus the nurturing is encouraged in a context of personal freedom as consonant with life in community.

5. Hope College has long valued intercollegiate cooperation. Whereas fundamentalist colleges have often sought to go their way in fierce independence, Hope has known the value of cooperation and joint effort. The College has been a member of the Great Lakes Colleges Association since the association's in-

ception in 1961. Hope is also a charter member of the Michigan Colleges Foundation (1949), and a member of several other cooperative ventures. Most recently it joined forces with Calvin College in establishing a joint nursing program.

Ringenberg's criteria are, of course, not the only possible gauge for measuring the status of a Christian college. But his criteria constitute a helpful "checklist" for sizing up a contemporary evangelical college and help to provide a brief characterization of Hope College.

III.
VAN WYLEN'S CONTRIBUTIONS AND VISION

This, in very broad strokes, is the history of Hope College and its "religious" nature. What was President Van Wylen's place in that history and in that Christian academic framework? What was his vision of a Christian college and of Hope College? How did he articulate that vision? How much of that vision did he achieve during his presidency?

Gordon Van Wylen was the ninth president of Hope College. He came to Hope in 1972, after the College had been without a president for two years. During his tenure Hope grew significantly in a number of ways.

The most visible growth was in the development of the campus. New buildings erected during Van Wylen's presidency include the Dow Physical Education Center, the College East Apartments, the Maas Student and Conference Center, the Gordon and Margaret Van Wylen Library, and the Admissions Office (the last two completed after his retirement but planned by Van Wylen). Buildings which underwent either expansion or major renovation include the De Pree Art Center, the Phelps dining area, the De Witt Center, Van Vleck Hall, and Voorhees Hall. The overall appearance of the campus was also greatly improved, especially by transforming 12th Street into a pedestrian mall.

This expansion and refurbishing obviously demanded great financial resources, as did the increase in salaries and the enlarging of the endowment fund. Although Van Wylen had expressed reservations about his ability to raise funds when he assumed the presidency, he became a very effective fund-raiser. The capstone of his financial campaigns was the successful completion of the Campaign for Hope, which closed on the day of his retirement, with an amount of over $31 million. Moreover, during his presidency the endowment grew from $2 to $20 million.

The College also flourished academically during Van Wylen's presidency. Although the President was usually not directly involved in the academic affairs of the College, he did set the tone and gave overall leadership for academic achievement and excellence. Hope continued its status as a nationally recognized college in the physical and biological sciences, and faculty achievement in other departments was outstanding as well. Hope faculty authored a substantial number of books during Van Wylen's years, some of national repute, and hundreds of journal articles. Outside financial grants to the faculty during these years increased greatly. Another major effort was the stress on faculty development and renewal. Van Wylen strongly supported programs such as the Andrew W. Mellon Foundation grant for faculty development and an extensive program of summer study grants, in addition to sabbatical study leaves.

Van Wylen was active in developing the administrative structure of the College as well. He introduced a system of appointing one academic dean for each division. Each dean was to have an office in an academic building, in order to maintain regular contact with the faculty, and the dean also had control over discretionary funds for each division. Van Wylen also streamlined procedures for appointing new faculty members and for granting promotion and tenure.

But Van Wylen's greatest contribution to Hope College was his affirming a vision and mission of Christian education. When the Board of Trustees sought a new president in 1971, the first qualification they listed was for a person "who will clearly define our mission."

Van Wylen took that charge seriously, and from his first to his last year he sought to delineate and embody that vision in terms of overall philosophy, faculty recruitment, and personal conduct. His aim went counter to that of many Christian colleges in the twentieth century, which weakened or dissolved denominational ties and muted their Christian voice. His aim was to make the College more explicitly Christian. This aim was not always shared by all the faculty, as some wanted a broader ideological framework and others feared that Hope was destined to become a Bible college.

Part of Van Wylen's aim was to promote a mutually supportive relationship with the Reformed Church in America. He did not favor a denominational college which would allow only RCA students or faculty, or which would be under direct control of the General Synod.

But Van Wylen did favor a genuine identification with the RCA. In his annual report to the General Synod, in his appearance at classis meetings, and in his talks and sermons to RCA congregations he sought to foster closer ties with the church's constituency. Even though RCA students represented less than thirty-five percent of the student body, and only about sixty percent of the faculty was RCA, Van Wylen felt that close identification with the RCA was both possible and desirable. This church had nourished the College for over a century, and such ties ought to be preserved. Moreover, Hope College would benefit from affirming its roots in the Reformed tradition and from receiving continued spiritual direction from a Reformed denomination. In turn the RCA would benefit from the cultural and intellectual stimulation provided by the College.

The charting of the mission of the College was a more complicated challenge, both because of the diversity among the faculty

and the complexity of a modern liberal arts college. A major in-
dicator of Van Wylen's efforts in this area are the essays in this
volume. From his Inaugural Address to his last State of the College message, Van Wylen sought to develop his vision of Christian college education and how Hope College would embody that
vision. Even though he did not construct an elaborate philosophic
statement on the integration of faith and learning, he did always
strive to hold up his aim of making Hope College intentionally
Christian, both in life-style and in its academic program.

This development of a Christian vision took different forms,
sometimes in stressing the personal, sometimes the institutional
dimension. Thus Van Wylen stressed the importance of personal
modeling of the Christian faith in daily walk, especially in faculty contact with students, and he frequently quoted one of his
favorite texts, Philippians 4:8. Or he emphasized the significance
of Christian leadership, in academia as well as the broader world,
and he explored the contours of servant-leadership. Other personal Christian dimensions included the vision of seeing academic work as a calling from God and the challenge of striving
for excellence in all one's life.

In promoting a Christian stance in teaching and research
Van Wylen stressed the importance of a theology of creation and
of humanity being created in the image of God. This view of creation was to serve as a spur to exploring God's world in all of its
dimensions and to prepare students for taking their place of service in the world.

One of the most challenging (and controversial) issues concerned the definition of "Christian"—how narrow or wide was
one to interpret this and what did it mean in terms of faculty
agreement? Van Wylen felt most comfortable with the phrase "in
the context of the historic Christian faith." This formulation did
place Hope in a (broad) historic Christian tradition, without being
sectarian, and it allowed faculty from a wide range of Christian
traditions to join the College. Of course, the "broadness" of the

phrase also prompted rather divergent interpretations, especially in terms of faculty recruitment. Van Wylen therefore sought to explicate the statement in several papers, most notably in the paper "What We Owe Our Institutional Heirs."

Van Wylen steered Hope College through a very troubled decade. Books describing American higher education in the late sixties and the seventies carry titles such as *Unrest on the Campus, The Power of Protest,* and *Campus Apocalypse,* as demonstrations swept college campuses and the counterculture often engulfed traditional academic pursuits. During this period Christian colleges often reacted in one of two extremes: secularization or legalistic withdrawal. Many religious colleges, both Protestant and Catholic, severed ties with their religious traditions and at times became indistinguishable from their state-school counterparts. At the other extreme, many fundamentalist colleges reacted by creating conclaves of rigid pietism and legalistic codes of behavior, trying to insulate their students from the world. Van Wylen's religious vision and commonsense values helped to avoid such extremes at Hope College. The College kept its equilibrium between moral relativism, on the one hand, and arid legalism, on the other. The Christian tradition was maintained in the overall tenor of the College, and relations with the parent denomination were kept alive.

As suggested above, only the future historian of Hope College will be able to assess the years 1972-87 in the history of the College and the significance of Gordon Van Wylen's presidency. At this point the College is very grateful for the many gifts he contributed so unstintingly and for his providing a clear direction for the College. A part of that gift are the essays which follow. They are recommended to our readers, both as a historical record of these fifteen years of Hope College and as the embodiment of a vision for Christian higher education.

Harry Boonstra
Elton J. Bruins

NOTES

1 Wynand Wichers, *A Century of Hope, 1866-1966* (Grand Rapids, Mich.: Eerdmans, 1968), p. 90.

2 Wichers, p. 112.

3 Wichers, p. 85.

4 The influence of the East was not limited to finances. The first two presidents and many of the teachers during the first twenty-five years of the college came from the East. One of the by-products of this eastern influence was the immediate use of English as a language of instruction.

5 Walter Hobbs and L. Richard Meeth, *Diversity Among Christian Colleges* (Arlington, Va.: Studies in Higher Education, 1980).

6 Hobbs, p. 12.

7 Hobbs, p. 12.

8 Merrimon Cuninggim, "Categories of Church Relatedness," in Robert Rue Parsonage, *Church Related Higher Education* (Valley Forge: Judson Press, 1978).

9 Cuninggim, p. 34.

10 Cuninggim, p. 35.

11 Cuninggim, p. 32.

12 Cuninggim, p. 34.

13 William C. Ringenberg, *The Christian College* (Grand Rapids, Mich.: Eerdmans/Christian University Press, 1984).

14 Ringenberg, pp. 195ff.

15 Not included in the version of "What We Owe Our Institutional Heirs" in this volume. See the original paper, subtitled, "A Report on the Future of Hope College," 1985, pp. 52-53.

16 Original paper, p. 56.

BIBLIOGRAPHY

Hobbs, Walter and L. Richard Meeth. *Diversity Among Christian Colleges.* Arlington, Virginia, Studies in Higher Education, 1980.

Parsonage, Robert Rue. *Church Related Higher Education.* Valley Forge, Judson Press, 1978.

Ringenberg, William C. *The Christian College.* Grand Rapids, Michigan, Eerdmans/Christian University Press, 1984.

Wichers, Wynand. *A Century of Hope, 1866-1966.* Grand Rapids, Michigan, Eerdmans, 1968.

The Lines Have Fallen to Me
in Pleasant Places

President Van Wylen assumed his duties at the College during the summer of 1972. On October 13, 1972, a solemn Inauguration was held, at which he presented his Inaugural Address. The address ranges over a number of issues, but focuses especially on the fundamental purpose of Hope College.

The change that has occurred in the climate, purpose, public acceptance, and vigor of colleges and universities in this country and throughout the world has been profound. Indeed, to view the scene of higher education is to be all but overwhelmed by the pressures and counterpressures that exist in it today. There are pressures of all kinds to change the internal practices of colleges and universities with the hope of ensuring their proper responses to the needs and aspirations of minority groups and of women. Some expect colleges and universities to be active (even hyperactive) agents in solving contemporary problems of war, poverty, disease, crime, environmental abuse, and racial injustice.

Others believe that the primary objective of colleges and universities is to train men and women to fulfill specific vocational and professional needs. Still others would use colleges and universities—destroying them if necessary—to achieve their particular goals for the world in which we all must live. To these pressures we must add the problems of internal management and governance, of public acceptance, of funding, and of the changing interests of young people. The role of the federal government in higher education is changing significantly, as evidenced by the recent passage of the Omnibus Higher Education Bill, which offers new promises as well as new perils. The financial plight of private colleges has been publicized and is familiar. It is in the light of all these considerations—these changes and these pressures for further change—that I address you.

I had hoped for the wisdom and vision to make some definitive comments with regard to higher education and the issues we jointly face. But in reviewing the voluminous literature and pondering the insights of persons who have combined great scholarship with experience, I realize that on these issues and at this stage, I am less a teacher and more a student.

Moreover, I believe that the diversity of our institutions, along with the complexity of the issues involved in higher education, may well preclude the possibility of statements that are definitive and universal. It is probably more appropriate for each of us, and specifically for us at Hope College, to consider these issues, pressures, and problems and then, in the light of our own history, traditions, and commitments, define our goals, chart our course, and pursue these with diligence. It is in this context that I would share with you certain thoughts, observations, and aspirations I have about Hope College.

I begin with a general observation. From a Christian point of view what we are is a more critical matter than what we do. The Christian's primary emphasis is on being rather than doing, on one's attitude rather than one's actions. In the Beatitudes we find that we are enjoined to be meek and merciful and pure in heart. The assumption is that if we are right in our inner being, the right actions will follow. Certainly this holds true for individuals; and, to some measure, it also holds true for organizations and communities. What we are as an institution is a composite of what we are as individuals; therefore, we can speak appropriately of the character and attitudes of such an organization and community as Hope College.

I submit to you that the basic characteristic of Hope College is our commitment to truth—its discovery, its transmission, and its application. That claim is neither unique nor profound, for every institution of higher learning would subscribe to it. The important question is how we at Hope, committed as we are to Christianity and to the liberal arts, perceive the truth. In answering this question we define our essential being.

As I was reflecting on this, I was helped by a booklet given to me by our distinguished chancellor emeritus, Dr. William Vander Lugt. This booklet, *Quid Est Veritas?*, by Albert C. Outler of Southern Methodist University, makes a helpful distinction between two kinds of truth. One he terms "discursive truth"; the other is the concept of truth that is denoted in the New Testament by the Greek word *aletheia*. Discursive truth is the kind of truth that can be discussed and verified by analysis, experiment, reason, or even by imagination. It embraces all academic disciplines, from mathematics and logic to the humanities and the fine arts. We come to know discursive truth through our comprehension of the intelligible patterns, structures, and values in the world around us.

At Hope, as members of a scholarly community of faculty and students, we are committed to excellence in discursive truth. This commitment requires that we be diligent, hardworking, imaginative, and constructively critical in every facet of our academic programs. Such excellence does not mean that we must be involved in every subject area—emphatically it does not. In fact, at Hope, as we think through our mission and goals, we must be selective in choosing the areas to which we will be committed. But such excellence does mean that once we choose to undertake an area of study or research, we will provide the resources, facilities, the personnel—not simply to fulfill our commitments, but to fulfill them according to our self-set goals. At Hope College we would be a fully participating member of the worldwide community of higher education; we can accept no alternative to the pursuit of excellence in discursive truth.

But at Hope College we are also committed to the other dimension of truth identified by Professor Outler. This is the concept of truth referred to in the New Testament in such phrases as "you shall know the truth and the truth shall make you free," and "grace and truth come to us through Jesus Christ." This truth is based upon the awareness that the ultimate reality in this vast complex in space and time in which we live is the personal, infinite God in whom all things in their final analysis have their origin. Basic also to this view of truth is the creation of humanity in the image of God. Our abilities to reason, to communicate, to create, and to love are reflections of the very nature and character of God. We were also created to live in a social context and to live in a mutually enriching and supporting relationship with our neighbors. Further, in this view, we have been given a unique role in this creation to act as agents of the Creator in tending and caring for the physical and biological environment in which we live. And even though sin and evil have entered and have marred our relationship to our Creator, to our neighbor, and to nature, this view still defines the fundamental nature of humanity and the relationships which are basic to a life of purpose and joy.

The New Testament view of truth also holds that through a decisive act of God, namely, the Incarnation—and all that this event encompasses in the life and death and resurrection of Jesus Christ—we can be restored in a significant way to this relationship to God, to our neighbors, and to nature. In coming to know our Creator, we find the freedom and joy he intended us to have, see ourselves and our mission from his point of view, enjoy the gifts in nature and culture that he has provided, and experience his Spirit in our lives. As Outler states, this truth is the "revelation of God's power to transform men's fears, guilt, impotence, and humiliation into a sense of security based on trust and confidence in God." This is the truth that gives quality to our existence and significance to all our learning. Throughout its history, Hope College has been committed to this truth with the same finality that has marked its commitment to discursive truth. A vigorous and continuing commitment to both will provide us with unique opportunities in a troubled world where basic questions of purpose, meaning, and future destiny are once again coming to the fore.

Institutionally, this dual commitment is our reason for being. It is a glorious one, but we must be aware that it poses special problems. We must avoid the temptation to place these two dimensions of truth at odds, one against the other. We must avoid such a temptation no matter how reasonable or how urgent the case may seem for elevating one over the other. Instead we must see them as complementary to one another, as warp and woof. Truth as presented to us in the New Testament brings us, through Jesus Christ, into a relationship with our Creator-Redeemer. Having the experience of him and constrained with his will, we are free to inquire into his creation and to discover all that is implied in the concept of discursive truth.

In trying to understand these two dimensions of truth, an analogy from physics may be helpful. There are certain phenomena involving light that are best understood by considering light to be a wave; other phenomena are best understood by considering light to be a particle. Although we may never be able to bring these two concepts together definitely into a single model, our understanding of light is greatly facilitated by using both concepts. So it is with truth. Truth is basically one; yet, by distinguishing between discursive truth and the New Testament concept of truth, we can more accurately perceive our mission as a Christian liberal arts college.

At Hope we are privileged to take serious account of both these dimensions of truth and to work out the full implications of both. The terms of the privilege are that we do so first in our own persons, so that within each of us there is a commitment to our Creator-Redeemer. The commitment is to fulfill his purpose in us and through us, so long as we live in his creation. Secondly, the privilege requires that we go outside ourselves to explore both aspects of truth in the various disciplines, professions, and artistic activities that make up the Hope College curriculum. This is a tremendous undertaking, one that calls for the best efforts of faculty and students, as well as the support and encouragement of all those who make up the Hope community. It also means that at Hope College we must preserve the atmosphere of freedom and trust that will enable us to explore in a creative manner both of these dimensions of truth.

At this point, I would like to address a few words particularly to students. Almost beyond the telling I have already come to enjoy the opportunity of knowing you, and I appreciate your friendship, your encouragement, and your dedication to excellence.

Regardless of your present spiritual commitment, I welcome you as valued companions in our search for truth. We do expect that you will master your academic program and leave Hope College with a sound grasp of discursive truth as it applies to the program you have selected. To those of you who have already made the full commitment implied by New Testament truth, I say, join with us in making this commitment an integral part of our lives and our academic studies. To those of you who do not share this commitment, let me say that unless and until you are honestly persuaded to share it, your right to refrain will be protected. But do be an honest seeker for truth and respond readily with mind and heart as you are able.

To all of you I submit that the essential character of Hope College offers us an exciting and challenging exercise. This, I believe, was what one Hope student was saying when he remarked that, "Hope isn't really a place, it's an ideal. Once you get caught up in it, you can't get out. It will change your whole life." In no other way can I account for the fact that Hope College—of humble beginnings, of limited resources, of small endowment, and located off the beaten path—has held a distinguished position in higher education for several decades. I pledge my best efforts to retain this essential character of Hope College, while doing my utmost to help it serve as an active participant in the modern community of higher education.

As I noted earlier, what we do springs from what we are. It is my conviction that at Hope College our basic character and commitment give us an invaluable opportunity to contribute to two pressing problems in higher education today. These are the problems of value and relevance—of that delicate balance between what we might call timeless concerns and timely concerns. In the rest of my remarks I would like to probe these two issues in turn.

Today there is much discussion regarding values and a renewed agreement that higher education must be value-oriented. Nearly everyone agrees on the need for values, but there is little agreement as to what should serve as a basis for our value system. At Hope College the basis for our value system is rooted in the two dimensions of truth that I have outlined. In all value systems, ours included, a primary element is one's perception of humanity—how we view ourselves and our neighbors—and what one wishes on behalf of individuals and society at large. The concept of truth I have outlined offers a tremendous view of humanity because it perceives us as created in the image of God. Our desire for ourselves and for others is that both individually and corporately we will achieve our potential and enjoy all the fullness of life that God intended for us. Yet both personal experience and worldly observation tell us that many factors prevent us from achieving this goal. Internally there is pride, self-pity, envy, and sloth; externally there is poverty, war, prejudice, and cruelty. Therefore, our value system must be one that takes account of one inescapable fact: All is not well with humanity and society. Fortunately we do not have to proceed to build from nothing, in total ignorance and confusion. Through our knowledge of the Creator and the reflection of his character as manifested in the creation, we are given insights that enable us to become the persons he wants us to be and to strive to make it possible for every other person to achieve the same.

St. Paul summarized this foundation for a value system in his memorable words to the Philippians (4:8), "Whatever is true, whatever is honorable, whatever is just, whatever is pure, whatever is lovely, whatever is gracious, if there is any excellence, if there is anything worthy of praise, think about these things." What a basis for eliminating every social injustice and for promoting that which will enrich and ennoble the lives of everyone with whom we come in contact. Since we have been created in the image of God, we take seriously the gifts and abilities with which we have been endowed and we aim to develop each person's fullest potential in art and music and drama. In so doing our aim is to enrich human life by the expression and enjoyment of that which is noble and pure. In all of this we must be realistic, admitting that the world harbors evil and sin that would lead us to degrade and misuse our endowments. But culture is also an integral part of the *redemptive* work of God in Jesus Christ and this provides an incentive to ensure that our cultural activities promote that which is honorable and just and pure.

It is also within this view of humanity that we can develop the concept of the Hope College community—a community permeated with integrity and compassion, which enables us corporately to develop whatever gifts have been given us. Any community that has a value system rooted in the Creator can achieve something of the fullness of life that God intended us to enjoy through corporate experience.

Since this value system is based firmly in reality, it necessarily has a direct bearing on a matter of great national and international concern—namely, our view of nature, our use of natural resources, and our preservation of the environment. According to this view of truth, all of nature and creation has value in itself and of itself because God made it. Thus painting nature can be just as "Christian" an exercise as painting a specifically religious or biblical subject. Because all of nature was made by God, it deserves to be treated with respect and dignity. This does not mean that all of nature is one, or that nature has no categories or orders. It does mean that we must treat all of nature with respect, that we must attempt to understand the relationships and orders in creation and take these into account to fulfill our responsibilities toward nature.

We note in the second place that although we ourselves are creatures and therefore part of nature, we have been given particular responsibility to care for nature and for the world. Thus we have two relationships—to the Creator and, as the Creator's agent, to all of nature and to the whole world, even beyond the boundaries of our planet. What has become clear in recent years is that we have not exercised this responsibility in a proper manner. Too often in letting our concern for material prosperity and pleasure determine our decisions we have failed in the exercise of our stewardship. In attempting to exercise it more properly we need to view nature from a biblical perspective—see that we can not only use nature to fulfill our needs and wants for food, shelter, clothing, beauty, and recreation, but that this can be done while we preserve the legacy it represents. Perceiving that sin and evil have touched nature itself—that it is frequently "red in tooth and claw"—we know also that the redemptive work of Christ needs to be applied to it. At Hope College we have the privilege of reappraising these responsibilities, not only to ensure survival for the human race, but as part of our calling to make this planet, like our lives, a source of joy and peace and love.

The question of values leads directly to the issue of relevance in higher education today—to what extent should institutions of higher education prepare students to perform specific functions, tasks, or assignments in society?

The question has become urgent for at least two reasons. The first is that students, as never before, have been questioning the relevance of their education in meeting pressing societal needs. Often this questioning stems from an ignorance of what scholarship is and from a failure to accept scholarship as valid in its own right on the basis of our relationship to God. And, therefore, on concluding that their education is not relevant to solving either their own problems or the global problems of the world, students often join the wave of anti-intellectualism that has swept across the higher education scene—either by dropping out or unenthusiastically pursuing their academic program because they can find no suitable alternative.

The second reason for this question's urgency is a pragmatic one: In many areas there is a severe shortage of jobs for college graduates. This shortage was dramatized last spring by a CBS television special with the title: "Higher Education—Who Needs It?" The job shortage has caused many young people—particularly those who view college as a vehicle for upward mobility—to question the value of all higher education. Here again is an issue that is clarified by our commitment to the two dimensions of truth.

The question of relevance places further demands on us, for there is work to be done and tasks to be performed in society. In regard to these workaday requirements institutions of higher education can take one of three points of view. The first is largely vocational and focuses on preparing students to perform specific functions in society—functions that are essential, honorable, and currently undervalued. The second is characteristic of our large universities that emphasize graduate education and research and focus on developing global solutions to societal problems. The development of polio vaccine or the design of new transit systems would be typical examples. Then there is a third point of view that is, I believe, unique to colleges like ours: to prepare students to assume major responsibilities in various areas and to function compassionately within these areas, striving to meet human needs and to improve the quality of life for all persons whom they encounter. This approach is summarized very well in a statement from Isaiah 50:4: "The Lord God has given me the tongue of the learned that I should know how to speak a word in season to him that is weary." This third view falls between the narrow scope of the first and the global scope of the second. It partakes of both the others, really, and can be expressed in industry, in government, in law, in medicine, in education—in nearly every institution and activity of society.

Thus at Hope College, our concept of a liberal arts education enriches our lives so that we can work in this world with a heightened sense of responsibility and compassion. Although we do not train students in medicine, for example, we do expect our graduates who go on to study medicine to bring a special something to their professional studies and later to their professional exercise. This special something is the mix of responsibility and compassion, of intellectuality and spirituality, of worldly knowledge and other-worldly aspiration that I have tried to describe.

This concept leads me to a final thought about relevance. I would like for us at Hope College to have a vision of preparing our students for leadership. In coming to know our alumni I'm struck by how distinguished a record for leadership we already have. And I have asked myself anew what the essential ingredients for leadership are. Certainly they defy generalization, though they are easily identified in action. They include a superior command of the subject matter at hand. They also include an interest in people and a commitment to insure that the leader's activity—whether in business, science, or art—is directed toward serving people rather than using them to further his or her own ends. Another ingredient is the leader's ability to see his own activity in the context of the whole—by which I mean the overall purposes and goals of human life. Finally, there is the personal requirement that the leader's personal life be marked by integrity, compassion, and a sense of purpose. All of these ingredients go into the making of leaders—the men and women that the world has always needed, but never more so than in these days when the possibilities have been so drastically enlarged—the possibilities for good, the possibilities for evil. I believe that all the factors that apply to Hope today—the kind of education we give, the scale on which we give it, the shared vision of our mission—conspire to help us prepare future leaders out of all proportion to our numbers and resources. By this I mean, of course, not only the headline makers, but also the kind of leaders who, quietly and courageously, make all the difference between a decent world and the sort of world this would be without the leavening of spirituality.

This, then, is the vision of how I conceive the character and mission of Hope College. It involves our commitment to excellence in discursive truth. It embraces our commitment to all that is implied in the New Testament concept of truth and to the integration of both of these conceptions of truth in our personal lives and in our academic endeavors. It results in a distinctive and dynamic basis for values and for relevance in every aspect of the life and mission of Hope College.

Finally, let me say that my unbounded enthusiasm for Hope and my optimism for its future are based on my belief that God has his purposes to accomplish through us. It is on this firmest of foundations that I know we will base our exchanges in the years ahead—praying and working together confidently and with joy.

Inaugural Address
October 1972

Leadership in a Troubled World

The President usually addressed the faculty and staff at the beginning of each school year, presenting both data on the coming year and often discussing a significant aspect in the life of the College. Here he mentions for the first time the question of the size of Hope College—a question which frequently recurs in later writings. Also, with hindsight, we see the irony of the assumption that the completion of the physical education building (later: the Dow Center) would probably be the President's first and last major building involvement. The sensitive question of tenure is broached for the first time.

This is a crucial year in the life of Hope College because of the situation in the world and the nation. There is the crisis in our national government which was brought into such sharp focus over the summer. Yet, even these events are in a measure only symptoms of much deeper and more fundamental issues—issues which relate to moral, ethical, and social questions. Thus we begin this year with a measure of dismay and discouragement in regard to our nation, and with great uncertainty about the future.

In addition to this crisis in government, there is the matter of inflation and cost of living. On the one hand this is an international crisis; it touches every nation and has profound implications for world trade and international relations. On the other hand it touches each of us personally and influences our daily diet and our own fiscal affairs. And, of course, it touches us as a college as we seek to manage our financial affairs, provide for the needs of our academic programs, respond to the financial needs of students, and provide an adequate and proper level of salaries. The great uncertainty about our economic future is a matter of concern as we chart our course for the days and years ahead.

On the world scene, there are still many conflicts, tensions,

and turbulent issues. While we can be thankful for the measure of
peace that we do enjoy, the Near East, the Far East, and Ireland
continue to be troubled areas which could readily become major
conflict areas. At home there are many matters which are far
from an adequate resolution—the cities, racial relations, the environment, and the energy crisis are but a few of the many matters that call for attention and solution.

I have not mentioned these national and international issues to
be dramatic or because I have any particular wisdom or insight
on the resolution of these matters, but rather because this is the
framework and background in which we must face some very important questions here at Hope College. I will outline some
aspects of our situation, as I see it, and thus set the stage for the
presentations which will follow.

One of these issues is the matter of the size of the College.
Since 1965 we have been operating on a long-range plan that the
College will grow to 2,600 students. At the time this was
adopted, there were many people who thought the better course
would be to hold enrollment at 1,800. Last fall the enrollment was
2,100, and this fall it will be about 2,000. Further, as we project
ahead, taking into account the numbers of high school graduates,
the fraction of these graduates who will go on to college, and the
number who will choose a four-year liberal arts college, it is clear
that further growth would be difficult to achieve, and that it will
require a diligent effort to retain our present size. It seems quite
clear that the years ahead will, at best, be years of very small
growth, that maintaining our present size is a reasonable prospect, and that there may be a small contraction.

I do not think that our enrollment of around 2,000 is to be la-
mented. In fact, there are some very positive aspects to this size.
Our present size is large enough to offer a wide variety of programs, both academic and extracurricular, and to respond to a diversity of student interests. Further, I do not believe that we have

overexpanded our campus facilities. If we can complete the re-modeling projects which we have planned, and construct a new physical education building, our campus construction will be essentially completed for a decade. This would mean that we could concentrate on maintenance and regular updating of our facilities. Finally, as I have come to understand the situation here at Hope College, we really have very limited financial resources. In the annual report which I have prepared for distribution to alumni and friends, I tried to point this out by comparing our endowment, enrollment, and tuition with a number of other schools. We simply do not have the resources of those schools with whom we would like to compete or with whom we compare ourselves. I believe it would be well to focus on increasing our financial base, so that we have funds to improve our quality, rather than increase in quantity. I believe that in so doing we can better serve the students, the church, and society at large. I find it a very exciting prospect to increase our financial resources so that we can simply do a number of things better than we can at present.

If we accept this premise that we will not increase in size, there are a number of questions which we must face. One of these relates to faculty staffing and tenure. Given the age distribution of our faculty and a constant enrollment, the tendency will be to arrive at a situation where a very large fraction of our faculty hold tenure. Such a situation would give rise to three major concerns:

1. It is necessary to retain considerable flexibility in a college such as Hope so that we can respond to changing student interests. We are all aware that these changes take place with considerable frequency. And even though we recognize that a liberal arts college is committed to an emphasis on teaching permanent ideas and lasting values, the fact is that we must respond in a measure to student interests and aspirations, and this requires flexibility in our staffing.

2. The cost of an essentially fully tenured faculty is significantly higher, simply because the majority of the staff will be in the upper salary ranks.

3. There is great advantage in bringing new faculty members into the College and into each department from time to time. The involvement of new faculty members brings new ideas, fresh evaluation, and new external contacts and associations.

In regard to tenure, there are at present two main areas of discussion in higher education circles. One is to find an alternate system and the other is to establish a definite limit to the number of faculty who can be tenured. In my judgment, the benefits of the tenure system are significant, and I have not learned of a system which is better, or even as good. For this reason, I strongly favor retaining the tenure system. But given the tenure system, there are three essential factors which must be kept in mind in effectively implementing it.

First, great discretion must be exercised in regard to who receives tenure. A decision to give tenure to a faculty member involves a commitment on the part of the institution of about $500,000 and a resolution that this is the person whom we want to influence some 6,000 lives. We must ensure that the faculty member who receives tenure has demonstrated ability to be a productive and effective teacher and scholar, not only for the present, but for the next three decades, and that this person supports and can contribute to the overall goals and development of the institution. Secondly, we must ensure that there is continual self-renewal of all faculty members so that they can be effective teachers and scholars throughout their entire academic career. Such is a very difficult achievement. But it is certainly possible, and I am encouraged by the enthusiasm which students frequently have for faculty members who have taught for thirty or more years and are in the last decade of their active academic careers. Finally, it would be well to develop an effective plan for evaluation of tenured faculty. In my judgment our present system is somewhat superficial and is too much tied to the annual salary increase. A thoughtful evaluation, in which the faculty member plays a major role in self-evaluation, which might take place once every three to five years, would probably be much more effective. It would be especially desirable if this evaluation could relate directly to the plans and activities which would occur during a sabbatical leave.

As to a limit to the percentage of tenured faculty, I do not believe it would be wise or necessary to establish a specific figure at this time. But I do believe that we should recognize that we would go beyond a sixty-five or seventy percent figure at considerable risk, and that we must be fully cognizant of the long-range impact of each tenure decision. This probably means that it will be more difficult to achieve tenure in the future. Our emphasis should be, on the one hand, to develop the strongest possible faculty for Hope College, consistent with our overall goals and objectives, and on the other, to be fair, considerate, and helpful to every faculty member. I believe it would be well to develop a pattern of offering two- or three-year appointments to new faculty members with the clear understanding that only a limited number of faculty members who hold such appointments will be reappointed to a second term, and that not all who are reappointed will eventually receive tenure.

I would also like to say a few words to those who do not have tenure and obviously aspire to do so. We recognize the difficulties of coming into the academic marketplace at this time, and we are sympathetic to your aspirations and want to do all we can to help you achieve your goal. It seems to me that the most essential aim is to demonstrate that you are indeed effective as a teacher-scholar, that you are a person who has the inner resources and drive that are necessary for continued self-renewal, that you are prepared to make the commitment of a tenured faculty member to promote the overall goals of the institution, and that you have your place in both the unity and diversity which are essential to the strength of the College. In effect, what I am urging is a convincing demonstration that you are the one to do these things, and that there is no need for us to look elsewhere—such is the surest way toward tenure for you and strength for the College.

Another concern relates to my opening remarks about the world as it is, and the role which Hope College can play. It seems to me that, as never before in my lifetime (and I hope this isn't simply a sign that I'm aging) there is a need for leadership and for a quality of life that promotes a sense of integrity, self-discipline, purpose, values, and compassion. Whether one looks at government, business, industry, education, the home, or the church, the need is very much the same. The end of the protest era gives us a tremendous opportunity to pursue with vigor academic programs and a total campus life that promotes such leadership and a life of purpose. And, if this is to be a significant dimension for campus life and activities, the impetus must come largely from the faculty. I hope that you share in this vision and will work to achieve it. A goal of leadership and purpose will mean the highest in personal ethics, which will influence common activities, such as the diligence with which we prepare for class, or how we counsel students. It also involves helping students to see the real excitement of looking at life and the world in its larger dimensions, and finding their own place where they can live and work with a sense of purpose and integrity.

Closely related to this is the need to develop a sense of community on this campus. We live in a world which is characterized by many tensions and much suspicion and distrust, where bugging and gossip and news leaks seem to be a way of life. It would be tremendous if we could develop a sense of openness, trust, and respect, and promote an environment where we guard one another's reputations, and promote one another's welfare. We all know how hard this is to achieve. We need to encourage each other in this regard.

One final thought. It seems to me that we might well have traveled in this past year, at least in this country, from an era of abundance and surplus to an era of scarcity. In such an environment there will be much questioning and much searching for alternative life-styles and value systems. This time offers us a tremendous opportunity to contribute to both the church and society as we seek to find lasting and permanent values, and to translate these into a creative, purposeful life, both individually and corporately. With our balance between the sciences, the humanities, and the arts, we are in a unique position to provide insights into relationships among these areas, and the integration of all of these facets into a broad worldview, in which material things have their place in relationship to truth and to lasting values and purposes.

In this regard I would like to suggest one specific possibility for interaction among faculty members. This would be to have, on a strictly voluntary basis, small groups of faculty, with no more than one from any department, who would meet together monthly for conversation, discussion, book reviews, and sharing of ideas. These groups, which would include spouses, would not only provide an opportunity for intellectual exchange, but would also enable us to know each other better as persons, and to share something of ourselves with each other.

What is it that gives us the courage to set before ourselves these noble purposes and goals, and believe that in this next year we can achieve, in a significant measure, a number of these goals? I enter this new year with considerable enthusiasm and confidence. We have so many things going for us—an excellent freshman class and an outstanding student body, a dedicated and effective faculty and staff, and many loyal friends and supporters. And yet, important as these are, our ultimate confidence is that these noble purposes and goals are the purposes and goals which God has given to us at Hope College. He will give us each the grace to be faithful and strong, and he will accomplish his purposes in us and through us. As we work this out in our personal lives and in the community, I believe it will be a rewarding and even an exciting year at Hope, particularly as we see the impact in the lives of students.

Faculty Retreat Address
August 1973

Dedication and Commitment

The Peale Science Center was under construction when Van Wylen arrived on campus, and was first used in the fall of 1973. The dedication of Peale took place on October 25, 1973, and was celebrated with the presence of many dignitaries, including Norman Vincent and Ruth Peale and the physicist William Pollard. In his opening remarks Van Wylen places scientific research and education in the context of Christian liberal arts education.

It is a wonderful privilege to have festive occasions to mark important events in the life and history of our communities and institutions. Today is such a day for Hope College: a day of joy and gratitude, a day to remember what others have done to make this event a reality, a day of dedication, and a day of looking ahead with anticipation. The trustees, faculty, and students of Hope College extend a cordial welcome to each of our visitors who are with us today.

Just what do we do in a dedication ceremony and what is the particular meaning of this service of dedication of the Peale Science Center? There are, I believe, two ways of perceiving this dedication. First, this is a dedication of purpose. Today we dedicate this building to our purposes in education—to education in the physical and social sciences, to research and the generation of new knowledge, to training in the techniques and skills which are required for scientific investigation, and to a better understanding of persons and of our social institutions. Such scientific purposes must be seen, of course, as part of commitment to a liberal education—to studying science in the context of the totality of life. That is, we dedicate this building as part of our commitment to be a Christian liberal arts college, to seek the unity in God himself, our Creator and Redeemer. Today we dedicate this building to these purposes and goals as we seek to fulfill our mission in education.

We also dedicate this building to God, or, to use the traditional phrase, "We dedicate this building to the glory of God." And of course, the dedication to God is closely related to our dedication of purpose. When we dedicate the building to the glory of God, we acknowledge God as the Creator, the Author of life, and our Father through Jesus Christ. Or, as Dr. William Pollard said in his lecture, we acknowledge the Lord as the Great Architect. Dedication to the glory of God also means that we seek to accomplish his purposes in every area of life. We acknowledge that he has so created us and placed us in this universe that we can learn and discover the wonders of his creation, and his purposes for us as we live in this world. He is the ultimate source of all of our scholarship and learning, and through him we accept our responsibilities in scholarship and education. Our purposes, our values, and our sense of the sacredness of life and the validity of scholarship find their ultimate source in God himself. And so, as we dedicate this building to the glory of God, we also dedicate the building to the noble purposes of higher education which have been set before us at Hope College. This is what makes today such a day of joy and deep personal happiness.

But in a service of dedication we must also look beyond the day of festivities. On Monday morning, when all our esteemed guests will be gone, what will take place in the Peale Science Center? How will we use this wonderful legacy? Let me share three additional thoughts with you.

The first use we will make of this building is to be involved in science—to learn the discoveries of the past and to gain some personal insight into the cumulative knowledge which has been discovered over the centuries. The departments which occupy this building cover some of the most exciting fields in science today—biology, chemistry, geology, and psychology. Knowledge in these fields is burgeoning. One of our major tasks is to help students learn and master the essential knowledge and discoveries of these fields.

And we are committed not only to *learning* science, but also to *doing* science. If there is one factor which has contributed much to Hope College's reputation in science, it is the emphasis on doing science—faculty and students together. The new Peale Science Center will enable us to do an even better job of this.

Our second goal is the use and application of knowledge to meet the needs and aspirations of contemporary society. Usually we do not think of discovery and application as coming from an undergraduate liberal arts college. Yet, one of the things which has impressed me on coming to Hope College is the significant practical research which has been done at Hope. It is exciting to visit a local manufacturer of equipment, which was designed on the basis of discovery and research at Hope College and which is now in the public domain. It is this kind of work, this creative problem-solving and the discovery of new knowledge, to which we are committed at Hope College. Students have the opportunity to participate in such activities while they are undergraduates and to carry such activity into their graduate studies and their professional lives.

Finally, we are committed to education both in the natural sciences and the social sciences in the context of the liberal arts. In the days ahead we will continue to seek to integrate scientific knowledge into a coherent set of values. And we will continue to seek to do so in the context of the Christian faith. We will help students majoring in science to develop a personal worldview in which science and faith are mutually supportive, and in which we acknowledge God as Creator and Lord.

Colleges sometimes assume that facilities in themselves can bring excellence in academic programs. But that assumption is a fallacy. The most essential ingredient in education, including scientific education, are the people involved. Of course, we are deeply grateful for this facility and for all those who made the Peale Science Center a reality, and to God, the Giver of all good and perfect gifts. And now the work in the building begins, and the excellence will be determined to a great degree by the people who work here. I know that I speak for all of the faculty and students involved, when I pledge that we will give of our best to use this building in pursuing the education and research for which it was intended.

Opening Remarks for the Dedication Ceremony
of the Peale Science Center
October 1973

Liberal Arts for Free Living

Although serving Hope College for a major part of his professional life, Van Wylen was no stranger to higher education generally. He was professor and later dean at the College of Engineering at the University of Michigan, and was involved in both state and national higher education in a number of ways. This general interest comes to expression in the commencement address at Grand Rapids Junior College. Here Van Wylen deals with the issue of vocational versus liberal arts education. But in this context also he reaches into his Christian heritage for an answer.

Mr. Runkel, Dean McCarthy, members of the graduating class of 1975, parents, husbands, wives, friends of the graduates, and members of the faculty:

It is a privilege for me to share this festive occasion with you. Graduation is a time of joy, and tonight I share your joy and extend to you who are graduating, and also to your parents, my congratulations and best wishes. It would be interesting to know the story of each of you—the efforts which you went through to complete your work, the growth in mind and spirit and maturity which has taken place in your life, and your plans for the future which have grown and evolved during your years at college. If we could know the story of each one of you, then we would begin to know the story of Grand Rapids Junior College.

I want to say a word of appreciation for your college. You no doubt hear Dean McCarthy and others say that this is one of the finest junior colleges in the country. You expect them to say this. But, as an outsider I share this same view. Grand Rapids Junior College has a tradition of excellence which has developed over many years, and which continues to this day. When I graduated from Ottawa Hills High School in 1937, when the impact of the depression was still with us, many of my classmates attended Grand Rapids Junior College and then entered the University of

Michigan in their junior year. They were as well qualified as those who had gone directly from high school to the university. That is the tradition of excellence of this college and in this you have had a part.

Tonight I would like to talk briefly about a matter which has frequently been on my mind—and perhaps on yours as well during your years in college. This is the question of liberal arts education versus vocational or technical education. Some of you are committed to the liberal arts, and will be going on to a liberal arts college to complete your studies; others of you have completed a technical program and will soon begin work. Perhaps there is even some tension between these points of view here at the college. Perhaps you have wrestled with the question of which is the right road for you. Is one more prestigous than the other? Is one more beneficial to society than the other? Are they mutually exclusive? And how does each fit into the complex society in which we live, and into a comprehensive worldview?

In some ways I faced these questions myself. My background is engineering, which is certainly a technical and rather pragmatic vocation. Yet, three years ago I became the president of a liberal arts college. Many have asked me about my qualifications for this position, and how I reconciled these two perspectives which, in the minds of many, are conflicting. And while serving as dean of the College of Engineering at the University of Michigan, I often wrestled with the question of the liberal arts component of an engineering curriculum.

I think one would have to admit at the outset that there has, in fact, been a conflict between the liberal arts and the technical perspectives. In seeking to understand why this developed, we must recognize that liberal arts education in the Western world has arisen primarily out of the classical Greek tradition. In this tradition human essence is understood to be mind or reason. Through the exercise of our reason we discover and contemplate the truth, particularly eternal ideas and values. Inner harmony of the soul is found through contemplation and reason. It is significant to note that this view developed in a society in which there were many slaves, and relatively few freemen, and liberal education was available only to the privileged few who were free.

In this context there was a great disdain for material things. The material was an inferior category, the things which slaves dealt with. It is interesting to note that of the many Greek gods, only one was less than handsome. He was Hephaestus (the Romans called him Vulcan), the fire god and metal worker who devised all sorts of wonderful works and useful objects. But it is significant that Hephaestus had obvious physical deformities—a badly dislocated hip, and frail, lame legs which were barely able to support his powerful, but malformed, torso. He was ugly and frequently a figure of contempt. When he left his workshop to move among the gods, they laughed to see such an awkward cripple.

This disdain for the technical arts was clearly expressed by Aristotle when he wrote:

> Occupations are divided into those which are fit for freemen, and those which are unfit for them; and it follows from this that the total amount of useful knowledge imparted to children should never be large enough to make them mechanically minded. The term "mechanical" should properly be applied to any occupation, art, or instruction, which is to make the body, soul, or mind of a freeman unfit for the pursuit and practice of goodness. We may accordingly apply the word "mechanical" to any art or craft which adversely affects men's physical fitness, and to any employment which is pursued for the sake of gain and keeps men's minds too much and too meaningfully occupied.

It was this Greek view, with its disdain for the material and the technical, and the exaltation of the mind and reason on which the traditional ideal of liberal arts and the university was built.

There is also a very different perspective which has developed, especially in the last century and a half. In this view the essential nature of humanity is that we are physical and biological organisms reacting to and interacting with our environment. This perspective is strongly related to science and technology. Technological education, as we know it today, is an extension of the type of education in which parents taught children to hunt, or to weave, or when to sow and reap; in a more advanced form, this education involved a master craftsman training the apprentice. In our more sophisticated world such education has evolved into technical training, and it has become an integral part of higher education. Many young people prepare for their life's work through this type of educational experience.

In this perspective our humanness will be achieved through a proper adjustment to and interaction with the environment. And who can deny that our interaction with the environment has been greatly improved through technology: automatic heating and cooling of our homes and workplaces; telephone, radio, and television for communication; health care available to many; synthetic fabrics available in abundance; ease of transportation in many forms, including travel at speeds greater than the speed of sound. From this technology countless numbers of people have become millionaires, and the masses live in a style of affluence undreamed of just half a century ago.

Out of this whole approach to the nature of humanity has developed a philosophy which runs counter to Greek thought. This is the philosophy of pragmatism and it is primarily an American philosophy which says that one knows in order to do, and it is by doing that one knows that he knows. And on this philosophy of pragmatism we have developed much of our philosophy of education.

Thus we have two conflicting philosophies—one stressing the life of reason and contemplation, and disdaining that which is material and technological; the other, stressing the pragmatic and technological, through which we can greatly alter and improve our interaction with the environment, and greatly improve the quality of life.

What shall we say to these competing views? Is there another view of reality and humanity in which this conflict is avoided and which yet adequately deals with both these perspectives?

Let me briefly sketch a view which I believe more accurately describes the essentials of our nature, and thus avoids the two extremes. In this, a biblical view, we are free, responsible persons created in the image of God. Our essential nature is active, not simply contemplative; crucial decisions involve our will, and not simply our reason; we achieve our humanness through loving obedience to God in responsible action toward our neighbors and the created world around us. The gifts of mind and reason are wonderful gifts indeed, but they are only one facet of our total being and not autonomous in themselves. The world in which we live is God's world, and our interaction with the environment around us can never be divorced from our relationship to God. Work, technology, and those things which Aristotle called "mechanical" have real significance because through them we can fulfill the responsibility which God has given us, and we express our obedience to God as we live in and interact with our environment. Technology has played a major role in enabling us to live in a society which is not based on many slaves and few freemen. However, the goal of technology should not be simply material success, and technology should never be carried on without concern for the preservation of the world which God created. The resources of energy and materials must be used with concern for their total supply and for the total human community. Thus technology becomes a valid human enterprise as we live in obedience to God.

In this view of man and woman as free, responsible persons, created in the image of God, there is also a very appropriate role for the liberal arts. As I noted, the liberal arts were originally considered as the activities befitting freemen. In our society we are all (partly because of the benefits of technology), to a very significant extent, free people. What a tremendous view of a liberal arts education—an education which is appropriate, and even necessary, for free people.

What, very briefly, do we mean by "liberal arts"? In the medieval curriculum, the liberal arts included two groups of subjects. The first embraced grammar, rhetoric, and logic, and the second arithmetic, geometry, astronomy, and music. Thus, at a very early date in liberal arts education, there was a great emphasis on variety and diversity. In fact, we can say that every area of knowledge presents the opportunity for the exercise of intellectual curiosity, and whenever such is undertaken voluntarily as a means of living a fuller life, it is part of the liberal arts.

But once we link this view of liberal arts with the view of humanity in a theistic context, the full potential of liberal arts becomes apparent. In this context the role of liberal arts is not simple contemplation, or reason in itself, but rather to perceive the design and harmony of the universe, with its hierarchy and interdependence, and with right human conduct as an essential part of its operation. In this context a liberal arts education will promote virtue and morality.

But how far we have departed from this lofty goal in our contemporary view of the liberal arts! Few would maintain that our liberal arts colleges strive, above all else, to inculcate virtue. Scholarship and the quantification of all knowledge make such an attempt seem almost anti-intellectual. We seldom ask graduates of the liberal arts if their education has made them wise and virtuous. But if we can once again catch this biblical and theistic view of humanity, we will have the basis for a great and significant renewal in the liberal arts.

There is one other matter which must be stressed about this perspective. In this view of humanity we recognize that the fundamental problem is not ignorance, as suggested by the Greek view, or lack of material things, as suggested by a technological view; rather, it is *sin* which separates us from our fundamental relationship with God, and mars our interaction with our neighbor and the world around us. Once this fundamental problem of sin is recognized, one finds that the fear of God does indeed become the beginning of wisdom. For in this view both the liberal arts and technology have their place, and the two perspectives can be integrated into a meaningful whole.

Now we can see that those of you who are completing the technical program can do so with a sense of fulfillment, because you are using the resources of this world which God created to meet the needs of humanity. And you have your whole life to continue to use your mind and your reason, as you live in both this vertical relationship with God, and in a meaningful horizontal relationship with your neighbor. Those of you in liberal arts have the opportunity to use the insights of history, literature, and the arts to contribute to the fulfillment of your responsibilities to God and to others. And you need not feel that a meaningful involvement in the work of this world is out of place with your commitment to the liberal arts. To me, this is what makes life exciting—to have a view of myself, of God, my neighbor, and the universe which permits me to live an active, free life, and to fully embrace both the liberal arts and technology.

If this sounded a bit like a sermon, I apologize. But, I know of no other way to achieve the wholeness of life for which we all long. May you find wholeness and joy in abundance.

Commencement Address,
Grand Rapids Junior College
May 1975

The Spectacles of History

The annual President's Report tries to capture the highlights of a year in terms of finances, buildings, people, and accomplishments. The 1974-75 Report does so largely by historical comparison. Drawing on a history of the College, A Century of Hope, *Van Wylen, in this excerpt, compares the current year with the early years of the College, focusing especially on financial resources and international education.*

I have just finished my second reading of *A Century of Hope,* the very delightful and perceptive history of the first 100 years of Hope College. This book, which was published in 1966 when the College celebrated its centennial anniversary, was written by Dr. Wynand Wichers, sixth president, who was associated with the College for more than sixty years.

As I finished, I was particularly impressed with two things. The first is that the problems which we face today are essentially the same that the College has faced throughout its entire history. The second is that the College has, and continues to have, a very distinguished record of accomplishment, particularly when measured by the lives and contributions of its graduates. It is evident that the College has always focused on significant goals and, as a result, the difficulties and adversities which had to be overcome became occasions for strength, perseverance, and inspiration. This is the tradition which we strive to carry on today. I hope that aim will be evident as I present this review of the 1974-75 academic year in the context of some historical observations.

One cannot read *A Century of Hope* without being impressed with the continued struggle in regard to finances. True, we do not now face the struggle to survive that the College did in the 1870s and 1880s, when faculty salaries were frequently in arrears. But finances have been a major concern throughout the history of the

College. There have always been three dimensions to this problem: paying the current bills; providing the needed physical facilities for the ongoing programs of the College; and developing the long-term financial strength of the College. One reason for the present strength of Hope College is that the College has always sought to provide a balance between each of these needs. This balance has been reflected once again during this past year.

We are grateful to every person, business, foundation, and church which supported the College this past year. What makes this support particularly significant is that, while we did receive a few large gifts, this level of giving was achieved primarily through modest gifts from many persons and organizations. It means a great deal to us to have so many people sharing in the mission and goals of the College. To each of these donors, many of whom gave from limited personal resources, we extend our deepest appreciation.

Our first goal in regard to finances is to operate each year with a balanced budget; this is a simple economic necessity for both the present operation and the long-term strength of the College. We were able to do so again this past year—the eighth successive year of operating with a balanced budget. This is particularly significant in view of the drop in giving to the Annual Fund, and was achieved primarily because of an increase in enrollment and careful budget control.

Our second goal is to continue to provide adequate facilities for the College—facilities that are functional, that involve minimal operating and maintenance costs, and that will contribute to the attractiveness and beauty of the campus. Our major effort during this past year has been the development of a specific plan and a coordinated effort to secure the necessary funds to construct a new physical education center. Because this major effort has been much on my mind, I was particularly impressed with the account in *A Century of Hope* of the efforts in the early 1900s to secure funds for Carnegie Gymnasium, our present physical education facility.

Rather than attempt to summarize it, I will quote this delightful account:

> The old gymnasium, built in 1862, was entirely inadequate to meet the growing need for facilities for physical education and athletics. In 1902, the students filed a petition for needed repairs and equipment, but the President explained that the structure was not worth repair and that he already had raised $4,000 for a new gymnasium. Not until three years later was President Kollen able to report to the Council that "upon the kind request of the Reverend Donald Sage MacKay of the Collegiate Church of New York City, Mr. Andrew Carnegie had offered to donate $20,000 for the purpose on condition that a like amount be added to the endowment...."

Since the original grant was insufficient, Kollen made another appeal to Carnegie and received an additional $10,000. The new building was erected at a total cost of $30,688 including $1,718 for equipment. Hope College was now the proud possessor of one of the finest gymnasiums in the State of Michigan. In connection with the dedication, Mr. Andrew Judson Kolyn of the Class of 1906 composed a song sung to the tune of "Tammany," which remained a favorite for many years.

There are many parallels between this account and our present situation. Seventy years later our facilities are "entirely inadequate to meet the growing needs for facilities for physical education and athletics"; we have resisted requests to spend additional funds for repairs on the old gymnasium, choosing rather to focus our efforts on constructing a new facility; many are assisting us as we search for benefactors who will catch this vision and make it possible to achieve this goal; the trustees have wisely decided that we will not proceed with construction until we have sufficient gifts and pledges to complete the structure; and, finally, we are quite prepared to name the building—and even write a new song—to recognize the donor of a new facility! One major difference between that day and this is simply the factor of 100; the estimated cost of our new facility is $3,200,000.

As I read in *A Century of Hope* the account of the construction of the very lovely President's Home in which my family and I are privileged to live, I was impressed with the difficulties encountered in its construction.

In 1884, the Synod met in Grand Rapids and made a brief visit to Holland on Saturday afternoon. The Synod expressed pleasure with the beauty of the campus and the progress that had been made over the years. They noted, however, that there was no residence for the President. Meeting in regular session in Grand Rapids, the Synod resolved that a residence should be erected. Thirty-one hundred dollars was immediately subscribed by the delegates. . . . Construction was begun and the exterior completed in 1887. But then funds ran out, construction stopped, and the house remained boarded up for several years. In 1889, the Council asked the Board of Domestic Missions for an appropriation to finish it. The request was referred to the Women's Executive Committee, who voted a donation of $1,000. The residence was finally completed in 1892.

Permit me, in regard to campus facilities, to share one other delightful quote from *A Century of Hope*. The following statement is from the Board of Trustees to synod in 1891:

Hope College must be out of the race if material improvement is not made in the very near future. It appears useless to make application to the Board of Education. This Board apparently must cease to be a source of income to the College. Would that a man of God, with silver wand, might touch our beautiful campus and give it a nucleus of buildings adequate for our growing needs.

While we would be delighted to find this man or woman of God with the silver wand, our real confidence and hope lies in the many men and women of God who share in our mission of excellence in Christian liberal arts education. They give generously, as they are able, to further the work which this College has been carrying on since the first students enrolled 113 years ago.

Our final goal in regard to finances is to build the endowment of the College, with a view toward providing resources for long-term financial strength of the College. In my reading of *A Century of Hope,* I was impressed that even during those difficult early years of the College, there was a determined effort to insure the long-term strength of the College by building an endowment. When President Philip Phelps resigned in 1878, the endowment was $47,000; when President Charles Scott resigned in 1893, it was $109,000; in 1913 the endowment stood at $451,000, and in 1938 it was $789,000. Today the book value of our endowment is $3,051,033, which, compared to that of many colleges similar to Hope, is very low. The result is that we necessarily are more dependent on student fees as the major source (78%) of our income. Yet, because we serve so many students from middle-class homes, we strive to keep tuition as low as possible. The final result is real economy of operation, and salaries for faculty and staff which are significantly lower than at comparable colleges.

Economy of operation in terms of efficiency is always desirable, but paying low wages and salaries is regrettable. To me, the greatest incentive for building the endowment is to have additional resources so that, with continued economy of operation, we will be able to pay equitable salaries to all who work at the College and yet have minimal increases in tuition, so that students from homes of modest means can continue to attend Hope College.

The second major observation which I made on rereading *A Century of Hope* is that even though the College, throughout its history, has struggled with financial problems, and even though there have always been needs for new facilities, and even though the endowment is very limited today, the College has had a remarkable record of achievement as measured by the lives and accomplishments of its graduates. And this is the essential mission of the College, the purpose of our corporate endeavors.

But how does one measure this achievement? Statistics regarding alumni are difficult to gather, and even then do not tell the full story. Yet, the data from 1916, the year the College marked its fiftieth anniversary, are impressive: the alumni numbered 561, of whom 310 were ministers, 107 teachers, 40 doctors, and 18 lawyers.

It is quite evident that in these early decades the primary focus of the College related to the learned professions of that era—the ministry, education, medicine, and law. These graduates had a remarkable impact on people and on the world. Many of our older alumni attest to the profound influence which these graduates of the first half century of the life of the College had on them.

But the world has changed dramatically since 1916; in almost every area of human activity there are needs and opportunities for educated women and men. The percentage of our graduates entering the ministry and education has certainly gone down, primarily because of the great increase in the number of students in college and the large number who enter other professional fields. The economic recession of this past year, and the tightness of the job market in primary and secondary education, have had a marked influence on the number of positions available to our graduates. In an effort to assist our students in this area, we have continued to strengthen our program and activities of the Office of Career Planning and Placement. We are encouraged by the fact that many of our graduates are finding positions of challenge, and we continue to be convinced that a liberal arts education, coupled with a realistic attitude toward a vocation, is an excellent preparation for work and for the totality of life.

One of the striking dimensions of the College during its entire history has been its involvement in international education and affairs. It is quite amazing that under the leadership of President Phelps, the first president of Hope College, the first Japanese student enrolled in 1868, just two years after the first students graduated from Hope College. Throughout the early years a number of other Japanese students, as well as students from many other countries, enrolled at the College.

However, up to World War II the greatest international impact of the College was made through the exceptionally large number of graduates who served as missionaries abroad. In 1941 it was reported that 140 Hope College alumni were serving in this capacity. But even more significant than the number was the quality of their service in medicine, education, and evangelism. Many writers, both secular and Christian, have testified to the distinguished record of these alumni. The current focus of world attention on the Middle East serves to remind us that long before there was great wealth in this area, a number of Hope alumni served with distinction in this part of the world.

These two dimensions of international education—students from abroad studying at Hope College, and students and alumni studying and working overseas—continue to be a vital part of our program at Hope College.

This past year we had an exceptionally large number of students from abroad studying at Hope. During the summer of 1975 we had two groups of foreign students on campus for an American Experience Program. Both the Japanese program, which this year involved 41 students and has operated for the past 11 years, and the German program, which involved 59 German youths and was held for the first time, proved to be very successful. We are delighted that our campus and facilities can be used for this purpose, for through these activities we not only provide a meaningful experience for these students, but enlarge our own international perspective and involvement. It is also significant that each year a few of these students return to the campus as regular students.

We believe that many of our students will have a greatly enriched undergraduate experience if these years include some study abroad. We seek to provide diverse opportunities, so that each student has the opportunity to choose an overseas experience which best meets his or her particular interests. These include a semester or a year in France through our Grenoble program, or in almost any country through the Great Lakes Colleges Association or the Institute for European Studies, special May term courses in Europe, or an academic program or work experience during the summer.

In recent years there has been a great increase in the number of opportunities our graduates have to serve overseas. We are delighted with the very significant number and remarkable work of our graduates who today are serving as missionaries in a wide variety of capacities. In addition to these, an ever increasing number of our graduates are serving abroad in business, diplomatic service, education, the Peace Corps, and many other capacities. The ease of travel, the rise of multinational corporations and international banking, and the increase in foreign services and activities of the U.S. government, lead to many opportunities for work and service abroad. It is essential that we maintain a strong international atmosphere at Hope College, not only for our graduates who will work and serve overseas, but also for those who, though living in this country, seek to fulfill their global responsibilities and live their lives with a mature, sympathetic, and informed view of the world.

President's Report 1974-75
August 1975

Reservations on a Drinking Proposal

The question of students' rights and privileges while living on campus is often a complex one, especially as one student's conduct many infringe on the rights of another. This issue is particularly volatile in reference to the use of alcohol. In 1976 the question came to the fore because the dean of students proposed a liberalizing of the College's rules. Van Wylen disagreed and stated his position in a letter, which was published in the student paper, The Anchor, *of February 13, 1976.*

The following is taken from a letter written by President Gordon Van Wylen to Dean of Students Michael Gerrie. In it, Dr. Van Wylen responds to the proposal written by Gerrie and three students that would allow students to drink in the privacy of their rooms.

On the matter of alcohol, I have very serious reservations about the recommendations you have made. In order to present my views as accurately as possible, let me first state some personal views, so that you will know the presuppositions upon which I base my conclusions:

1. The use or non-use of alcohol is in itself not a matter of right or wrong. Non-use is not, per se, more Christian or more right than the use of it. Use or non-use of alcohol is a matter for individual decision.

2. Dependence on alcohol, and certainly any excessive use, does have moral and ethical implications as regards our body, our impact on others, and our ability to fulfill our mission and purpose in life.

3. We live in a time of both great stress (due to such factors as economic and social pressures, the rapid rate of change, and other stress factors) and of much dependence upon excessive use of alcohol. Stress and dependence upon alcohol are, no doubt, closely related, for many turn to alcohol, and use it excessively, as a re-

sponse to the great pressures which we experience in contemporary society.

4. Problems associated with the use of alcohol constitute some of the most serious social problems of this day. Many social workers believe that it is a far more severe problem than drugs. While we cannot change the world by our policies at Hope, we should strive to prepare our students to live responsibly in such a world.

As I have sought to examine the implications of this proposal for us at Hope, I believe there are several things to bear in mind:

1. The college years are a period of considerable stress. The approach which students take to handling stress in college will certainly bear on their ability to handle stress during all of their lives. One of the great things about a residential college, and particularly one which seeks to take Christianity seriously, is that it is a supporting community. This is the best approach to stress that I know, and one which we should strive to develop here at Hope.

2. For most students, the years at college, and particularly the first few years, are a crucial period of transition from home to life as an individual. During this time there is great need for a supportive environment. I certainly do not support "in loco parentis," but the alternative to this is not complete "laissez-faire."

I believe we should strive to develop a supportive environment in which students can make decisions without undue social pressure, evaluate and test the wisdom and consequences of these decisions, and so promote the fullest and noblest personal development.

3. We live in a crowded, fairly closeknit community—1,500 students within a couple of blocks. None of us can be totally isolated anywhere, but certainly not at Hope. What any one student does in a residential hall certainly influences others. Some rules (such as those relating to noise) are made for the benefit of the larger community, and this is certainly appropriate. In your memorandum you

acknowledged that a balance is necessary between the rights of the individual and the rights of the community. I fully support this.

4. Our primary goal is excellence in undergraduate, liberal arts education. This has implications for mind, body, and soul. Since we are a residential college, the experiences of students in the residence halls are a vital part of their education. Decisions which are made about our residence halls ought to be made with this primary goal in focus, yet keeping in mind, of course, the rights of the individual.

How do all of these observations come together in regard to an alcohol policy? In my judgment, after considering the proposal you have made, and other alternatives as well, I have concluded that our policy of prohibiting the use of alcohol in the residence halls or on campus is the best course of action to follow. My reasons for this are as follows:

1. I believe that this policy, among all other alternatives available, will best promote the development and maintenance of a supportive, concerned academic community. One of the distinguishing characteristics of Hope over the years has been that it is such a community and the result is found in the lives and accomplishments of our graduates. We have the responsibility to continue to develop and strengthen such a community and environment.

2. I believe that this policy best prevents easy dependence upon alcohol among our students.

3. I further believe that this policy best promotes the development of an environment where we can achieve our overall goals with a real degree of excellence. I am convinced that our academic goals, our programs in intramural and intercollegiate sports, theater, and music will be more fully accomplished if we maintain our present policy of prohibiting the consumption of alcohol in the residence halls.

4. Many different decisions, made over many years, have gone into making Hope the academic institution and community it is

today. It is impossible to determine the full significance of any single decision which has been made in the past, or to fully ascertain the future impact of a decision we make today.

Yet, we are called upon to estimate, as accurately as we can, the consequences of the decisions we make today. It is my conviction that the proposed change in policy regarding consumption of alcohol in the residence halls, would significantly change, and not for the better, the character of the college. This would not be an immediate change, but rather one which would evolve over the years, and make its impact upon the goals, the personnel of the college, and the nature of our community.

Thus, I have come to the conclusion that our present policy, among all the alternatives available, is the policy which we should continue to follow.

In your memorandum you state that the primary reason for the recommended change in our policy regarding alcohol relates to the issue of individual privacy and the problems this poses for enforcement in relation to the policy itself. I deeply respect this right of individual privacy, and wish to comment on it. Let me first comment on individual privacy as it relates to the policy itself, and then comment on the matter of enforcement.

If we make clear what our policies and regulations are in regard to our residence halls (including the prohibition of the use of alcohol), students who decide to come to Hope and live in the residence halls have a commitment to abide by these rules. The right to individual privacy is within the context of the rules which were in force when they made the decision to come to Hope and live in the residence halls. All of our policies should be made clear to students before they enroll at Hope and choose to live in the residence halls, for when they decide to come, they accept these policies. This does not, of course, mean that a student cannot urge that these policies be changed. It does mean that they cannot base their argument on a violation of their individual privacy.

Enforcement of any college policies, when necessary, must of course be done within the context of all the rights of a student to individual privacy. Where there is evidence (legitimately gained, of course) of a violation, we should treat this in the same way we treat violations of any other policy. This will involve confrontation, use of appropriate counsel, helping students to understand the rationale for our policy, and, if necessary, discipline.

I recognize that this may not be easy. But, let me outline a vision which I hope will be shared with many others and which could provide a framework for wide acceptance of our present policy on the use of alcohol in the residence halls.

What I long for, and am willing and anxious to work on as diligently as possible, and with all the strength and wisdom I have, is a college which has as its central focus the promotion and development of all that is noble and good, and the most exciting and wholesome development of the whole person—body, mind, and soul. One reason why I am so anxious to complete the new physical education center is the opportunities this will afford all students for the development of physical fitness and health.

I long to have a residential system which has good facilities, where students have the opportunity and take the time to think, to converse, to be alone, to pray, and in so doing to prepare to live vigorously in a world where stress and tensions abound. I am prepared to work diligently with you, your staff, and students to achieve this goal, for I long very much to achieve it. In my judgment, the proposed change in the alcohol policy would do nothing to achieve this goal, but would, in all probability, make it more difficult to achieve.

In my response I have not based my conclusions on the possible implications of the proposed change in our alcohol policy on giving to the college or on recruiting students. Personally, I believe they would be substantial and negative.

It would certainly not be prudent to make this change without thoroughly studying these implications and deciding if we are prepared to accept them. However, I much prefer that we make our decision on the basis of what we deem is the best decision to achieve this goal, and this I have tried to do.

February 1976

Mortar, Money, and Mission

Convocations are a time to inspire students for the new school year and to keep them abreast of new developments in the College. When reading these addresses chronologically, it is interesting to see the ongoing process of planning for new buildings; each year there is a somewhat different plan as new developments occur. Finances are an ongoing concern as well, but this also must be considered in the larger mission of the College.

It was at this meeting four years ago that I spoke for the first time in a formal way to the faculty and students at Hope College. I recall quite vividly how nervous I was that evening. I was expected to set forth my thoughts regarding the future of Hope College. I was very new to Hope College, having arrived on campus just a few months before the opening convocation. I had much to learn and I was ill prepared to give a definitive address.

Tonight I'm grateful for the four years which I have been able to spend at Hope College. I appreciate the encouragement, counsel, support, and friendship which I have received from so many of you. My thanks to each of you for the part which you have played in my life and the life of the College during these four years.

This evening I would like to share with you my vision for Hope College. I would stress that this is not a plan which is cast in concrete; it is not even a blueprint. Rather, it is a vision which I hope we can discuss, refine, expand, and more fully articulate in the days and months ahead.

SIZE OF THE COLLEGE

Let me first share a few thoughts with you about the future size of Hope College. This fall we have about 2,150 full-time students and about 200 part-time students; we will have about 1,600 students in our residence halls. Essentially all of our facilities will be used to their full capacity.

It is my conviction that Hope College should remain at its present size. We are large enough to have diversity in our academic programs, strong cultural programs, such as music and theater, which offer excellent opportunities for participation by both majors and non-majors in these fields, an intercollegiate athletic program of excellence for both men and women, and many opportunities for research and personal development. Yet we are small enough to retain strong personal relationships between faculty and students and within the student body. Our present size is such that we can offer a coherent, integrated program in liberal education to all of our students—and, certainly, coherence and integration is becoming increasingly important in a world which is fragmented in so many ways.

Further, our present enrollment effectively matches our campus facilities. Any expansion in our enrollment would require additional facilities, and this in turn would call for substantial funds for construction. Moreover, the number of high school graduates will drop significantly in the years ahead. It is for these reasons that we should limit our enrollment to our present level, and focus our efforts on the further development of the college in other ways than an increase in size.

In the question of enrollment I do want to touch on our commitment to minority students. In the late 1960s and early 1970s, there was a strong impetus to increase the number of blacks, Hispanics, and other minority groups on our campuses. Often this impetus came in the context of demonstrations, sit-ins, or other pressure tactics. The tactics might at times have been poorly chosen and more extreme than necessary, but the need was real. I am grateful for the progress which was made in offering opportunities to minority students in those years.

Now some of the external pressure is gone. But I would like Hope College to continue a vigorous pursual of these goals, not because of outside pressure, but because of our own convictions and commitment. I believe that our goal should be to have a college where every minority student is fully accepted in every aspect of the life of the college. I believe that Hope College can offer our minority students a fully integrated college experience. This is not to say that there should not be opportunities for special activities or groups for blacks or Hispanics. But such activity should always be by choice, and never by default on the part of the rest of us because these students are not fully integrated into the life of the College. The same relates to such areas as black and Hispanic and women studies. Our goal should be to fully integrate these studies into our academic programs, so that they will become an integral part of the curriculum for all of our students. I urge all of us to do our part in building a community in which each person is fully accepted and can participate in every aspect of the life of the College.

CAMPUS FACILITIES

Most of you are well aware of our plans to construct the new physical education center. A committee of faculty, staff, and students has been working with the architect for the past eight months, with the result that a very functional and attractive facility has been designed, including a dance studio. We hope to break ground in November, and we expect the facility to be fully ready in about twenty months. At this point we are seeking to raise the last $400,000 we need for this building.

I want to express our appreciation to the faculty and students who have contributed resources to make this facility possible. Two years ago our students conducted a campaign and raised about $25,000 in pledges from students. I think it is a mark of the quality of the students we have at Hope College that they gave generously to provide a facility which they would not personally use. This is the spirit which makes Hope such a great place.

Our next major projects will be the renovation of Voorhees Hall and Carnegie Gymnasium. As soon as the new physical education center is completed, we hope to initiate the planning phase of these projects. Our tentative plans are to relocate the administrative offices, which now are in Van Raalte, the art department, the education department, and perhaps one of the other departments now located in Lubbers Hall, into these two renovated and perhaps expanded facilities. [EDITOR'S NOTE: Carnegie Gymnasium was demolished in 1982, and Voorhees Hall is now a student residence hall. The departments mentioned have all found a home elsewhere.]

Another high priority is the development of some green areas around the campus. We very much need this space for informal recreational activities. These areas will significantly improve the overall appearance of the campus, and are part of our overall campus planning.

One other matter of concern is the development of our residence halls. It is of vital importance that these facilities, and the total environment of the residence halls, be conducive to our overall purposes. The residence halls must be good places to study and live, which requires well-planned and well-cared-for furnishings in the rooms, as well as adequate study areas and quiet areas in each of our larger residence halls. We will be giving these matters careful consideration in the years ahead.

LONG-RANGE FINANCIAL PLANNING

In our financial planning we also must keep our overall mission in mind. Our goal is twofold—to have excellence in every aspect of the College, and to make this education available within the financial resources of our students.

Our commitment to excellence means that we must have a faculty and staff and facilities which will enable us to achieve this goal. Implied in this statement is a commitment to pay adequate and competitive salaries to all those who work at Hope College. And all of this means adequate financial resources for the College. However, our goal is also to make a Hope College education available to every student who is admitted, regardless of the student's financial resources. Such a goal does not mean that it will require no sacrifice to attend Hope College, but it does mean that we must keep the costs to attend Hope College within reach of our students. We must therefore have the lowest possible tuition and an adequate program of financial aid.

Some people in private higher education are looking primarily to government support at the state and federal level to solve their financial problems. A number of programs have been established which provide significant support for our students and for the College. One of the finest of these is the Tuition-Grant program which Michigan and many other states have adopted and from which many of our Michigan students benefit. Unfortunately, most of these programs are not transferable to colleges outside of the state in which they have been established. This is particularly hard on a college such as Hope, where we have substantial numbers of out-of-state students. One of the greatest steps we could take in higher education would be to make such Tuition Grants transferable, so that they could be used wherever a student chooses to attend college; as a college we would strongly support such a move.

A number of independent colleges have taken an opposite position and decided that they will not accept any government support; they feel that in this way they will be exempted from much government regulation and will be more free to pursue their objectives and goals. I confess that on occasion, as the bureaucracy and regulations increase, I am inclined toward this position.

However, in my judgment this is too simplistic a solution. If we choose, as a nation, to support science education through the National Science Foundation, I see no reason why Hope College should not receive these funds for its science programs. It is a much greater challenge to solve the problem of excessive regulation and control than to withdraw from any involvement and leave the problem to others. Programs of financial aid which go directly to students, and give students the freedom of choice, rather than direct aid to institutions, is one way to approach this matter. Such programs should receive the support of Hope College.

Yet, having said this, I wish to reaffirm my conviction that the basic approach to our long-range financial needs must be from private rather than from government sources. We had a very successful year last year, with $2,600,000 received in gifts from private sources, which include alumni, parents, friends, foundations, churches, and business and industry. This amounts to $1,200 per student. How grateful we can be for such generous support. Our future strength will depend on the continued and increased support from these private sources. In the years ahead we will also be seeking to build up the endowment of the College and use this income to achieve our goals of excellence and reasonable costs.

OUR LARGER GOALS

All of these concerns about which I have been speaking, such as facilities and finances, are not the ultimate concern of the College. These are only the means to achieve our larger goals. Even though these are difficult concerns, in many ways they are easier to deal with than the larger issues, such as our overall purpose and how we will achieve such a purpose.

Let me state as simply as I can what I perceive as our mission. I consider our mission to be excellence in undergraduate residential liberal arts education, within the context of the Christian faith. This has been the historic mission of the College and continues to be our mission today. The means and implementation may change, but our basic purpose remains.

Let me first share a few thoughts about the world in which we live and in which we must achieve our mission. Much has been written about our contemporary world, and in these few minutes I cannot begin to offer a comprehensive analysis. Yet, all of us recognize that we live at a time of great questioning of established institutions and values, of tremendous worldwide problems relating to race, the availability of energy and natural resources, the population explosion, hunger and starvation, and the distribution of wealth. War on some scale seems always present and the threat of nuclear war becomes increasingly real as more nations have the capacity to produce nuclear weapons. Very significant intellectual questions are being raised about the nature of humanity and of ultimate reality, questions which deal directly with our understanding of who we are and the meaning and purpose of life. In these days there is really very little optimism for our long-range future. At best there seems to be the attitude of muddling through for the present, with the vague hope that in the long run things will get better.

It is in this context that we as a college and each of us as individuals must seek to achieve our goal. In spite of the dark picture I have just sketched, I still have real optimism for Hope College and for our part as faculty and students, both in the life of the College and in our world. I have this optimism because I believe we have something very significant to contribute, because I consider the world and time in which we live and work to be both exciting and challenging, and because I believe we have a message of hope and of significant purpose.

I believe such optimism and hope is justified, because I hold that each person is a child of God and that God has richly endowed us with the gifts of body, mind, and spirit, the capacity to love and be loved, the ability to think, to reason, to judge, and to create. He has given us the gifts of love and marriage and sex and children and homes. He has given us the capacity to work, and study, and learn so that we can unravel some of the secrets and more fully understand the created world around us. God has given us the gifts of music, art, and drama. He has given us all these gifts to enrich our lives and to enable us to enrich the lives of others, and to acknowledge him as the giver of every good and perfect gift.

It is this understanding of God and ourselves that gives the real dynamic to a liberal arts education. In this view every subject and every aspect of life has significance and is worthy of study because it has its origin in God. Further, in our studies we do not start from scratch, but appropriate and build upon the cumulative wisdom of humanity through the ages. We are the recipients of a great treasure.

Paul wrote some words which sum up very well this view of life: ". . . whatever is true, whatever is honorable, whatever is just, whatever is pure, whatever is lovely, whatever is gracious, if there is any excellence, if there is anything worthy of praise, think about these things" (Phil. 4:8).

From this view on life and reality, three thoughts emerge which are directly relevant to us as we consider our mission as a liberal arts college.

First, the whole world is open to us to study and to enjoy. We are surrounded by an abundance of good things which are worthy of our study, our time, and our energies. God calls us to find real fulfillment as we discover his world, and his place for us in that world.

One corollary follows directly from this perspective. The real significance and joy of life does not consist in the abundance of things which we possess. Many of us, and particularly those of us who are younger, may very well live much of our lives with a significantly lower standard than we have today. Yet, such a change has the potential of forcing us to rediscover the more important gifts which we have been given. The perspective on life and education which we find in the liberal arts can be the basis for developing a meaningful life which is not dependent on an abundance of material things.

Secondly, this view of life does, in a very significant way, diminish the distinction between the sacred and the secular. Everything has been created by God, and as those who have been created in the image of God, all of this universe is open to us. We do, of course, exercise a sense of stewardship and responsibility in the world; we are called to care for and preserve and wisely use all its resources. We exercise this responsibility not only to preserve the human species and to improve the quality of life, but also to fulfill the purpose which God has given us in this world. It is in this sense that the distinction between the secular and the sacred disappears.

Thirdly, we do not exercise these responsibilities each by ourselves, but as part of the human community. I do not need to recite to you all the ways in which human relationships are being broken these days. The greatest indictment of our present society is the broken relationships in every area of life. Instead, I want to focus our vision on what God intends for us—to live in a community where there is mutual concern and compassion, where we can join together in developing our creative and artistic skills, in doing our study and research, as well as recreation and sports, and, above all, in uniting for worship. Hope College exists to be such a community; each of us, as faculty and students, has the privilege of being a member of this community and enjoying all that it affords us.

We can make this idea very concrete in yet another area. One of the questions which is much on the minds of many students is what kind of a job you can get after graduation. This is a very important question and one which certainly warrants careful consideration. Yet there is a perspective within the view of life of which I have been speaking which looks beyond professional success. We also see the tremendous opportunities to live a life of significance and service—in prison reform, in business, in the arts, in politics, in science, in medicine, in the ministry. We can see ourselves as recipients of all these great gifts, and then plan to use them to accomplish something of God's purpose in the world.

And how does all of this tie in with a liberal arts education? In this education we do not prepare so much for a specific job as we do for life. A liberal arts education is intended to instill in us the ability to learn and the joy of learning, to gain at least some understanding of the great treasure of knowledge and culture, to know God and to know ourselves, to learn to communicate, to think clearly, to develop a coherent value system, and to make decisions in the light of this value system.

It is as I catch this vision of life and reality, perceive our world in the light of this vision, and see each of you as a child of God, endowed with all these gifts, that I really become excited about the potential and mission of Hope College. I trust that we will have many opportunities to talk about this vision, and work together to make it a reality.

Convocation Address
August 1976

Mission in Action

In 1977 Van Wylen formulated a concise mission statement for the College: "To offer academic programs of recognized excellence in the liberal arts, in the setting of an undergraduate, residential, coeducational college and in the context of the Christian faith." He and others frequently used this statement in the coming years to help define the purpose and goals of Hope College. Here that statement becomes the context for discussing admissions, leadership, and a number of other issues.

In this report I would like to share with you some of my deeper concerns for Hope College. Matters involving finances and physical facilities are of vital importance and require diligent attention and much hard work. They are, however, in essence only the tools to achieve our larger purpose. The central mission of the College is carried on by you, the faculty and staff, in your daily interactions with students.

At this time last year I presented to you a statement of my understanding of the mission and purpose of Hope College. Formulating that statement was a very good exercise for me and I am grateful for the acceptance which this statement of our mission has received from many members of the faculty and staff of the College. At that time I tried to develop a single sentence statement of the purpose of the College: "To offer academic programs of recognized excellence in the liberal arts, in the setting of an undergraduate, residential, coeducational college and in the context of the Christian faith." Using this statement as a starting point I would like to present to you some observations and concerns about our individual and corporate responsibilities as we seek to fulfill this mission in the years ahead.

The first matter I would like to touch on is admissions. Issues in admissions are of vital concern to all of us, and a successful admissions program is essential to our fulfilling our mission. This is a strategic time to address this matter because our new director of admissions will soon be assuming his responsibilities.

There are both quantitative and qualitative aspects to our admissions program. Our goal is to have enough applications so that we can be assured of operating at the full capacity of the College, which, in the light of our mission, involves retaining the College at its present size. Few things would be of greater help to us in the overall administration of the College than to be assured of having the enrollment maintained at this pre-planned level. In recent years we have had just enough applicants to achieve our desired number of students and we have never really been sure of our enrollment until registration day. It would be of great help if we had a modest excess of applications so that we could be assured of maintaining our level of enrollment.

This quantity is closely related to the matter of quality. We have, in my judgment, a very significant number of outstanding students. We also have many students who, though not falling into this category of excellence, have been very satisfactory students, and have gone on to do significant work after graduation. I also believe that we have too many marginal students (in relationship to our mission) and that a decrease in the number of these, and an increase in the number of excellent students would be very beneficial in fulfulling our mission.

To accomplish these two goals, namely, assuring the level of enrollment and having a larger number of superior students, we should set two specific aims:

1. To increase the number of applications by 200. This increase would allow us to be somewhat more selective and also insure that we can maintain our present level of enrollment.

2. To initiate a modest but carefully designed program of institutional research, directed to learning more about our students as they enter, how they achieve at Hope, and what factors most significantly influence them. The purpose would be to provide feedback

to the admissions program as well as to guide us in the development of our academic program and in counseling.

Just a word about FOCUS. I believe that we should continue our FOCUS program. The primary purpose should be to give the opportunity of a Hope education to students who have definite potential but an inadequate high school record for regular admission. The emphasis should be on giving the students this opportunity and not on reaching our enrollment goals. The number of students admitted to the FOCUS program should be limited to the number we can handle effectively. However, we do need some good research so that we can better identify students for the FOCUS program who have good potential for success.

There are many facets to an effective admissions program. The matter of effective publicity nationally, as well as at the state and regional levels, and a good financial aid program are essential elements. We have an excellent financial aid program and we are giving increased attention to the matter of publicity. We have also been giving considerable thought to the possibility of increasing the number of scholarships which are awarded solely on the basis of merit. We have found that students are very responsive to these, even though in most cases the scholarships are fairly small.

Just one final point. You as faculty members are among the most valuable resources we have for our admissions program. Many of you have been of tremendous help to us and we are deeply grateful to you. Under the leadership of our new director of admissions we will continue to seek ways in which you can effectively participate in our admissions program.

The second matter I want to touch on relates to budgeting and the use of our resources. It is really quite amazing as one goes through the budgeting process to realize how little freedom we actually have. Heat, power, other utilities, maintenance, debt service, and salaries for faculty and staff account for the major portion of the budget and are essentially fixed. The result is that we have very little flexibility in responding to new opportunities and needs or to changing priorities. A vital factor in determining our effectiveness is the way in which we allocate those limited resources over which we do have control. Which is more important—an additional faculty position, library acquisitions, faculty travel to conferences, equipment replacement, a new vehicle for maintenance, or an increase in salaries? These are the kinds of decisions which, though very specific and often relatively minor at the time, do influence the College very significantly in the long run. To make these decisions effectively we very much need your input as faculty and staff members, as departments, as representatives of various special programs and needs.

One of the great joys of being in administration is to be able to repond to such needs and in so doing to see the work of the College prosper. Your thoughtful input, particularly as it is documented and given in the light of the overall needs of the College, is essential. We assure you of our continued efforts to respond as effectively as we can in the light of the overall operation of the College.

I would also like to share some thoughts regarding our commitment to excellence. There are many tangible ways in which our commitment to excellence is evident throughout the College. I sense this in our academic programs, in our scholarly endeavors, and in our development program.

In recent years this commitment has also become increasingly evident in the appearance of the campus. From time to time I wrestle with the question of what the budgetary priority should be for the beauty and appearance of the campus. I do have the conviction that for many visitors, including prospective students and their parents, the appearance of the campus is one of the most effective ways to communicate our commitment to excellence. This is much more tangible to visitors than words about academic achievements, and can effectively underscore our overall commitment to excellence.

There is a matter related to this commitment to excellence on which I do have a concern, that is, the sense of courtesy, grace, and manners in the life of the College. There was a time when the emphasis on manners was an essential element of campus life. Jackets, ties, and dresses were worn for dinner, and the meals were served in the dining hall with considerable emphasis on manners and courtesy. All of this changed radically in the late 1960s and early 1970s. Perhaps some change was needed. Yet I have the feeling that we went too far and that we lost something very vital and important in the process.

At this point I have no specific suggestions or proposals to make, but I do want to call this concern to your attention and ask you to give it your consideration. If anything is to be done, it will be done largely through the faculty. Even then it will come about, not through a formal program, but as our commitment to excellence in manners and grace is expressed in the life-style that each of us practices and in our expectations for students. The residential life of the College can also play a vital role in this emphasis upon manners and graces.

One of my primary reasons for being so anxious to accomplish the expansion of the dining hall is that I believe that this will help us to promote manners and more gracious dining on the part of students. Our experience has been that new facilities do promote a more thoughtful and gracious life-style. As we improve our facilities and as we set high standards for ourselves and our students, we have a special opportunity to make significant progress in this area.

In closing I would like to touch on some thoughts regarding our commitment to the Christian faith. I have been grateful for the many creative and thoughtful ways in which our Christian commitment is finding expression on campus. This is a source of encouragement and inspiration to me and to many others.

Recently I have been thinking about one particular facet of this commitment, that is, Paul's injunction about our not being conformed to the world but being transformed by the renewal of our minds. The implications of this for an academic institution are profound, because we interact with so many facets of contemporary life and society. I find in my own work that it is easy to simply accept contemporary standards and procedures, without trying to think through the implications of our Christian commitment. I know that many of you have been wrestling with these matters as well.

Rather than discussing this issue abstractly, I will present a few specific matters and through these raise some relevant questions.

1. My first concern is the nature and role of leadership. In this country we have a great tendency to glorify the manager, the leader, the successful person. This tendency is practiced to extremes in professional athletics and the entertainment field, but finds strong expression as well in business and politics. Yet, in the Christian perspective, the central thrust is that being a leader involves serving, and success is not to be measured in material rewards or public acclaim.

We often stress the fact that we prepare our students for leadership. Perhaps we should emphasize more fully the servant nature of leadership. If we did so, we would, no doubt, have to think through more fully than we have to date just what this means. I suspect that we would find that many basic principles of management are still valid, but that the emphasis on being a servant relates to our overall goals and the way in which these management principles are implemented. This is a matter which will require careful thought but will be very exciting to do.

Recently Professor Barrie Richardson prepared a preliminary proposal for a program in servant-leadership for business students. As I read this, the thought came to me that perhaps we could enlarge the scope of this program and develop a four-course sequence, available to all of our students, on the principles of management within a Christian perspective. Many of our students will assume leadership and management positions in various fields. How good it would be if they had some understanding of the basic principles of management within a Christian context.

2. I will mention another matter very briefly because we have already given this considerable attention. This is the matter of athletics. One of the tragic developments in contemporary society is that athletic excellence has become professionalized and a source of earning amounts of money that greatly exceed the benefits to society. The result is a gross distortion of values in the minds of many young people and older persons as well. Here is a crucial area in which we can bring to bear Christian perspectives and alternatives. Much of what I have said about athletics could be readily extended to the entertainment field. I am not so much interested in our writing or talking critically about what is taking place as I am in providing alternatives which reflect a mature, thoughtful, Christian point of view.

3. My third concern relates to the efforts to increase our endowment to $10,000,000. I believe that our motive in seeking to accomplish this goal, which is to keep the costs of attending Hope College within reasonable bounds, is fully valid within the context of our Christian commitment. However, I am aware that historically many colleges, as they increase their endowment, decrease their interest in the church and their commitment to the Christian faith. I don't think a $10,000,000 endowment, relative to our size, is a great danger, but we could become vulnerable. And could we handle a $50,000,000 endowment? Would this make us think that we can be independent of the church, or of our constituency, and of God? I believe that increasing our endowment has the potential of being a very valuable resource to further our goals and to help us fulfill our servant mission. However, I want to avoid doing so simply because other colleges

are doing it. What does "transforming of our minds" have to do with increasing our endowment? I will welcome your thoughts and comments on this matter.

Much is written these days about the resurgence of evangelical Christianity and there is much to be thankful for in this movement. Yet, I believe that the world still needs persons and institutions who can thoughtfully, carefully, creatively, and graciously work out the implications of the historic faith for contemporary society. This is a truly great opportunity for us here at Hope. We have tremendous opportunities to do this in every facet of the life of the College—in our residence halls and campus life program, in intercollegiate and intramural sports, in our cultural activities, in our business practices and compensation programs, in our academic programs and the scholarly and more popular writings of our faculty.

It is in the light of this and all the considerations I have shared with you this morning that I find I am truly excited about the new academic year. There will be many challenges and many problems, and also correspondingly great rewards. As we work together in mutually supportive relationships we can, with God's help and grace, have another excellent year in the life of the College. Thank you for your part in this mission in the year ahead.

Faculty Conference Address
August 1978

Hope Even in Despair

In Hope College history 1980 will be remembered as the year of the fires. On April 28 the historic Van Raalte building went up in spectacular flames. A week earlier Van Vleck Hall, in the final stages of renovation, had suffered from a major fire. How did the College respond?

Knowing of your keen interest in the renovation of Van Vleck Hall, we thought we should present as soon as possible a full account of the fire that occurred April 21, and the action we have taken to begin immediately to repair the damage and to complete the renovation.

Two things stand out as I reflect on this event. The first is the remarkable change in attitude from Monday, the day of the fire, to Tuesday. The mood of sadness and even despair that prevailed on Monday is understandable. Watching this historic building being consumed in flames was a shocking experience in itself. But to see the water-logged contents from each room being removed, to think of the potential loss of a semester's work and of priceless mementoes, and to consider the disruption of moving to a new housing situation with just three weeks left in the semester, and the uncertainty of just how each student would cope—these thoughts created an even deeper sense of concern, compassion, and sadness.

But what an amazing change took place by Tuesday. Many concerns and hurts remained, of course. But a remarkable number of residents were coping very maturely with the situation. By Tuesday morning the decision was made to begin reconstruction immediately, and by late that afternoon, workmen were already on the job. The prevailing attitude was that this very tragic and disruptive event would not deter us from fulfilling our individual and collective missions. We would indeed go forward even though we faced substantial difficulties.

The second impression that remains is the extraordinary way in which so many people in the College community rallied to help. Students and staff worked diligently to remove personal belongings from the building while the fire was underway; the custodial and maintenance staffs worked late into Monday evening to remove the remaining contents. Above all, fellow students were supportive of each other in countless ways in helping to cope and to recover from a very difficult situation. I believe you would be proud of the way the entire campus community, and particularly the residents, have conducted themselves in this difficult situation.

A ceremony of rededication of Van Vleck Hall had been scheduled for Alumni Day on May 10. We have decided to continue with the ceremony, but to change the focus from Van Vleck Hall to a rededication of ourselves to the mission of the College to accomplish God's purposes of truth, grace, compassion, and justice through this great institution. Thank you for your part in the work of the College.

News From Hope College
May 1980

A Vision for Diversity

In the 1980s the student bodies at many colleges became more diversified, or at least colleges became more aware of the needs of the "non-traditional" student. Hope College also responded to a more diversified student body.

For the past several years, I have used this occasion to present a report on the state of the College. The primary purpose is to outline, as accurately as I can, the overall situation of the College, and thereby provide a basis for discussion and specific decisions as we work creatively and effectively together to accomplish our mission in the year ahead.

THE FUTURE OF HOPE COLLEGE

Let me first share with you some overall thoughts and impressions I have about the College at this time. Actually, these are a mixture of opposing thoughts, and they reflect the various issues and concerns that I wrestle with as I seek to provide stable and judicious leadership for the College.

On the one hand, there is a sense of well-being, a feeling and conviction that things are going well at Hope. We have not faced the financial crises that many other colleges have in recent years; enrollment has held up remarkably well; a good spirit of cooperation and mutual support prevails on campus. Many of you, as well as many visitors to the College this summer, have told me that the campus has never been more attractive and beautiful. The renovations we have finished on Van Vleck and Voorhees have added much to our sense of continuity with the past, and the plans we have for campus development are challenging and exciting. We have balanced the budget, the endowment is growing, and our constituency is genuinely supportive. Often, therefore, a

67

sense of well-being, satisfaction, and gratitude fills me and I can
continue to work with enthusiasm and confidence.

But then I look at other factors and I have a feeling of concern
and uncertainty. There is great economic uncertainty for the future. Will there be continued or even increased inflation? Will
there be a major economic crash? Will our donors be able to continue to give generously, which is so necessary simply to keep up
with inflation? Will we be able to raise the funds for our new
facilities? And what about enrollment? We are entering the period of sharp decline in the number of high school graduates.
Other colleges are competing vigorously for students. On the one
hand, there are prestigious colleges that charge much more than
we do that are attractive to many students. On the other hand,
there are publicly supported institutions, many of them very excellent, that charge far less than we do and are also attractive to
many students. The competition for outstanding faculty members
also remains keen. Superimposed on these concerns are all the
uncertainties in the international scene, with the almost unmen-
tionable threat of nuclear war continually hanging over us.

I sometimes ask myself if the period of success and accomplishment, which we have all enjoyed so much in recent years,
will soon come to an end. Is this, then, a time for great caution, a
time to be very conservative in our planning for the future?

I have not fully resolved the dilemma of these two perspectives, and I admit to some vacillation in my attitudes from day to
day and as specific issues arise. But, let me share a few ways in
which I have tried to resolve these conflicts and views and to
move forward with confidence. This resolution has two components.

The first is a significant measure of confidence in ourselves.
We have excellent facilities, a wonderful tradition and heritage,
outstanding, dedicated faculty and staff, and loyal supporters in

our alumni and friends. We have a well-defined mission and a good understanding of who we are as a college. There is considerable evidence that many parents and students are looking for a school such as Hope. With all of this, our task is to work diligently, creatively, and efficiently. The College has overcome many formidable obstacles in the past, and we can do so again as new or unusual problems arise. A look backward, and at our present resources and strengths, coupled with a commitment to diligence in the years ahead, is a great source of strength and encouragement.

The second way in which I have approached a resolution of this dilemma is, in essence, a theological one. Our primary responsibility is to educate, to the very best of our abilities, the students God has entrusted to us, and to fulfill his expectations of us in scholarship and support work. This is the essential purpose of the College, and we need to focus our primary energies and attention on this, believing that God will provide for our needs, that he will send the right students in the right number, and use us to enable them to grow and mature into the persons he calls them to be. Our primary calling is to be faithful to him and to his calling for us, and to work out the full implications of what it means to acknowledge Jesus Christ as Lord and Savior in our individual lives, in the Hope College community, and in our teaching and scholarship. Thus, we have a source of inspiration and strength outside ourselves, a resource freely available to us.

And so, as I wrestle with all these uncertainties about the future, I seek to resolve my doubt and concern with a renewed dedication to do my best, and to give such leadership that we will all do our best, and at the same time to trust and rest in the sovereignty and grace of God. It is this approach which is my overriding perspective for the new academic year, and the source of my confidence and optimism for the days and years ahead.

SPECIAL STUDENT GROUPS

And now to some more specific matters, especially as they relate
to certain student groups.

First, let us look at the presence of minority students at Hope.
Many of the black and other minority students who have studied
at Hope have, overall, had good experiences here and have gone
on to significant careers and accomplishments. There have, regrettably, been minority students who have not had a good experience at Hope. In some cases, this has been primarily an
academic problem, while in other cases it has been social or personal. However, I believe that we could significantly increase the
number of minority students at Hope, and ensure that we are
doing our best to enable each of these students to grow and mature as they develop their gifts and abilities.

There are several ways in which we can address this matter. I
would ask each unit on campus, such as admissions, student affairs,
and the academic departments, to give this matter diligent attention,
and to develop specific plans and recommendations. The Office of
Student Affairs should continue to meet with these students, listen
to them, give encouragement and counsel, and strive to create an environment where every activity (choir, theater, athletics, fraternities,
sororities) is equally accessible to every student on campus. I would
also ask the boards and committees to consider this matter, as far as
their own scope of activities is concerned. Could you, at one of your
meetings this fall, formulate plans and recommendations that will
enable us, as a liberal arts college committed to the Christian faith,
to better fulfill our responsibilities to these students, to society, and
to the church?

A second concern relates to our role to serve what has been
called "the non-traditional student." These students include those
who have been out of high school for a number of years but have
not started or finished college, those who have completed college
but would like to study areas of special concern at this point in

their careers, and those who would simply like to study for the sake of their own personal development.

As a College, we have taken the position that our central commitment and inherent strength must be as a coeducational, residential, undergraduate college dedicated to excellence in liberal arts education. We have always tried to avoid serving non-traditional students as a way to bolster our enrollment or solve a financial problem. Our commitment to non-traditional students has been to serve them. I believe this should continue to be our central emphasis.

However, given this view, I believe that we can still do much more to serve these non-traditional students as we give them encouragement, provide counseling, and schedule courses at times that most easily meet their needs. It will also be important to publicize these programs adequately.

Closely related to this is our concern to serve high school students. As you know, for many years we have had a program whereby local high school students could take a course at Hope during their senior year, with the high school, the student, and Hope College each paying one-third of the cost. We were concerned, however, to improve our service to the Holland community, so we decided to increase the amount the College would cover to one-half of the cost and to limit this to one course per semester. The schools will pay one-fourth of the cost, with the parents paying the other one-fourth. These courses are available to students on a "space available" basis.

Closely related to this is another concern I have had, and this is to offer some student courses, probably not for credit, to junior high and high school students in the summer. I am particularly thinking of courses in art, dance, computers, and physical fitness which would enhance these students' overall experience and development. This program would offer particular potential to ninth and tenth grade students, who tend to be too young to work and too old to play. I would welcome your suggestions on this possibility.

A VISION OF CHRISTIAN EDUCATION

I would like to conclude with some observations on how our commitment to the Christian faith should impact on the various facets of the life and work of the College.

At the outset, I want to say that I am grateful for the quiet, gracious ways in which the Christian faith permeates the life of our community. I sense this as faculty and staff members relate to students, as students relate to each other, and as many faculty and staff members and students reach out to persons in the community. Your Christian commitment is also manifest as you introduce, in appropriate and thoughtful ways, Christian perspectives and values into the courses you teach, your scholarship, your conversations with students, and your own life-styles, commitments, and attitudes. And, of course, your commitment is also evident in the more formal ways in which you worship on campus and in the community.

There are, however, some concerns I have. I wonder how we can be more effective as Christians, particularly in view of certain trends in the world in which we live. I would like to comment further on two of these.

The first of these concerns relates to two major movements in contemporary society. On the one hand, we have organizations such as the Moral Majority and an apparent resurgence of a rigid fundamentalism. Taken issue by issue, I resonate with many of their concerns and with their basic beliefs. But the failure of the group to put these beliefs and commitments into a larger, reasonably coherent worldview, and their tendency to impose their beliefs on others in a rigid, doctrinaire way, lead me to the conclusion that this movement is not for me. I often fear that overall this movement may well be more harmful than helpful to the church, to the Christian faith, and to society. Let me cite one example. Belief in the Creator is central and basic to the Christian faith. However, the word that tends to be used today is "creationism," a subtle shift with profound implications. Such examples can be multiplied over and over.

At the other end of the ideological and theological spectrum are the thoroughly non-theistic presuppositions that permeate so much of the thought and scholarship in universities and contemporary culture. Much of the pessimism, lack of commitment, and nihilism of contemporary society is rooted in a non-theistic understanding of life and reality. This, too, is a philosophy with which I cannot identify.

It is in contrast to both of these views that a mature, thoughtful understanding of the Christian faith—of a Creator-Redeemer who stands at the center of creation and life and who has come to us through the Incarnation—offers such a significant alternative. As we know our Creator, who is also our Redeemer in Christ, our perspective on all of life changes and we are inspired and strengthened to achieve the fullness of life he has called us to. We can be grateful that there are many scholars, educators, and leaders who share these views and can be of great help to us.

The opportunity and challenge before us is to let the full depth and impact of this mature understanding of the Christian faith permeate our lives in all that we do. The possibility of making significant contributions in this regard at Hope really excites me.

Closely related to this is my second concern. The issues we face in contemporary society are staggering. I don't need to recite them to you; they impinge upon us in every telecast and newspaper. How can we address these as responsible educators, scholars, citizens, and Christians? And how do we respond in our personal lives to a society in which values and standards seem so far removed from those that we understand to be our Lord's standards?

This, to my mind, is also a very exciting challenge. It seems to me that the starting point must be to work this out in our own lives first of all. And here we can be of great help to each other through example, discussion, encouragement, and fellowship.

And we cannot help but be observed by students, whether we like it or not, and be models for them. But we also want to work this out in our life as a community in our relationships with one another as we become considerate, supportive, sensitive, and disciplined persons with the conviction and courage to promote and to practice what we believe.

It is also important to think through the great principles from a Christian perspective on such issues as justice, mercy, work, resources, the role of government, and the family. Such consideration necessarily involves Christian theology and biblical understanding, as well as history and literature and philosophy, to mention only a few specific areas. How exciting Hope College can become if we believe and are convinced that we have something significant, transforming, perhaps even radical, to offer contemporary society.

I have only scratched the surface on this topic, and I would welcome the opportunity for broader discussion on this entire matter. I have thought of the possibility of our arranging a meeting, for those who are interested, for a day or two between New Year's Day and the start of the second semester, to discuss some of these issues.

These, then, are my perspectives on the College as we start a new academic year. I look forward to our life and work together. Thank you for all you are and for all you will be contributing to the College and to your students during this year. I wish you the very best in all you do.

State of the College Report
August 1981

A Quantum Step
to a New Level of Excellence

A college board of trustees is responsible for the overall direction of a college, but is also concerned about details of finances and buildings. In 1982 Van Wylen challenged the Board of Trustees with a bold vision and then spelled out some of the details of working out such a vision.

Sixteen years ago Hope College celebrated its centennial, climaxing a most remarkable century of growth and development. The founding of Hope was in itself a remarkable event. "Bold," "foolhardy," and "a great step of faith" could all describe the idea that the Holland Academy, then just five years old, with Van Vleck Hall as its only significant physical facility, could be expanded to become a four-year liberal arts college. But this is, in fact, what happened, and four years later, with its first graduates launched into the world, and a charter in hand from the State of Michigan, Hope College was officially launched.

The history of the first century, with its countless struggles and difficulties, has been well told in Wynand Wichers's *A Century of Hope.* Throughout the century there were periods of remarkable growth, when specific decisions or events moved the College to new levels of achievement. Several periods, usually fairly brief, were marked by significant development of the physical facilities of the campus. On other occasions, there were decisions that had a profound impact on the life of the College. One of these was certainly the building of Voorhees Hall as a residence for women, as this made it possible for Hope to become a truly coeducational institution.

During the first century, the College survived two world wars, several depressions, including the Great Depression of the 1930s,

numerous financial crises, and the pranks and escapades of undergraduates who in countless ways never really change.

The celebration of the centennial in 1966 launched a new commitment to growth and quality at Hope. A master plan for campus development was prepared; the Board of Trustees was
reorganized to ensure more effective management and leadership
on the part of the board; and the Second Century Club was organized to encourage generous support. In the early 1970s, the
board launched the Build Hope Campaign, a bold approach to
campus development and to building the financial base of the
College. The decade of the seventies was a period of implementation of these plans, and as a result we arrived at the decade of the
eighties with a fine campus, a strong faculty, good enrollment,
both as to number and quality of students, and a reputation for
academic excellence that has been built up over the years.

Just as we were ready to rest a bit in terms of campus development and to focus on building the endowment and furthering the
academic excellence of Hope, the disastrous Van Raalte Hall fire
occurred and we were again faced with the prospect of further
campus development. A new master plan for campus development was prepared, and we are well launched on this endeavor.
Already we can begin to perceive how truly excellent the campus
will be when this plan is completed. And even though much remains to be done on this project, it seems appropriate that we ask,
"What is the next quantum step beyond this that the College
should take to enable us to achieve a new level of excellence?"
This seems to be a particularly strategic time for us to ask this
and some related questions. What is the essence of this next step?
What is the vision we have for this new level of excellence?
What is the source of the strength and dynamic needed to achieve
it?

In my mind, this will be first and foremost a step which, for
want of a better term, I would call a step forward in spirit. The vision for this new level of achievement, and the dynamic to ac-

complish it is drawn from the wellspring of our lives, that provides a vision for that which is noble and true, and that motivates us to pursue this vision with vigor and confidence, both individually and as a College. This wellspring is, of course, God himself, and the faith we have in him.

One of the greatest strengths, and perhaps the greatest single strength of Hope over the years, has been a mature, thoughtful, wholehearted commitment to the Christian faith. This faith has implications for us personally for every facet of culture, scholarship and learning, for justice, mercy, and compassion, for the concerns and commerce of the world, and for personal freedom and responsibility. Ours is, of course, a Trinitarian understanding of God—God the Father, the Creator and Sustainer of this universe and the author of life; Jesus Christ, our Lord and Savior; and the Holy Spirit, who works and moves among us in ways we seldom perceive or understand and who makes the Father and Son personal and real to us.

BASIC PERSPECTIVES

There are three perspectives on education that are brought into focus when higher education is rooted in such faith in God. These will become increasingly evident and significant if we pursue this new level of excellence in the spirit and dynamic of the Christian faith. These three perspectives are:

Stewardship of the World

If this is God's world, it is worthy of our best efforts to know it, to understand it, to care for it, and to use its resources carefully. And if we have been created in the image of God, we have a special responsibility to exercise this stewardship, and to use the creative powers God has given us to further that which is noble and true. Further, because we bear the image of God, and have been and continue to be active participants in ongoing culture, the works and history of humankind over the centuries are worthy of our study and understanding. And if God has redeemed this world in Jesus Christ, we need insight and understanding as to how God's redemptive purposes have been accomplished in the past, and from this we must catch a vision as to how this can continue to be accomplished in our own day.

Personal Wholeness and Purpose

One of the remarkable things about the Christian faith is its balanced emphasis on objective truth and subjective experience. When applied to education, the emphasis on truth and stewardship referred to above is balanced with an equal emphasis upon what we are as persons—on the inner qualities of our lives, on the values we adopt for ourselves, and on our relationships with both God and our neighbor. Education at Hope must continue to have this balanced emphasis and perspective—a love for truth and knowledge in every area of life as well as for that personal wholeness and integrity which comes from knowing God. Wisdom, which is a much richer concept than knowledge, implies that we know ourselves, who we are and where we are going, as well as having an informed understanding of the various disciplines. That early Christian confession, "Jesus Christ is Lord," has profound implications for us personally, as well as for our perspective on truth and scholarship.

Focus on Serving

The biblical view that this is God's world, and that we have been redeemed in Christ, carries with it the emphasis that we have been called to serve. In this perspective, leadership is placed in the context of serving, and private ownership, while clearly established as legitimate and proper, carries with it the higher concept of stewardship, rather than autonomous ownership. In very real ways we are our brother's and sister's keeper, and as regards our own lives, there are values and issues and relationships that are worth striving for and, if necessary, dying for. In this perspective, therefore, education is not an end in itself, or a means to further our own desires or goals, but rather an opportunity to serve and thereby find a higher and nobler calling.

Such perspectives on education run counter to much contemporary thought and practice in education, though I believe they do reflect the deeper longings and aspirations of many persons in higher education. What a tremendous contribution Hope can make to higher education if we can achieve a new level of excellence by building on these commitments and perspectives.

In the following sections of this report, I have delineated more fully some implications of this approach to achieving a new level of excellence and have also made a number of specific suggestions and recommendations.

COLLEGE ARENAS

Academic

Hope is already strong academically, and we enjoy an excellent academic reputation. In what ways, then, can this renewal of spirit influence the academic life and work of the College?

I see this renewal, first of all, as ensuring that we preserve our present strengths. These strengths certainly include the very personal nature of the educational process at Hope, our emphasis on a content-oriented curriculum with modest, but not undue opportunities for experiential learning, and our commitment to a strong liberal arts base for all the majors we offer, as well as liberal arts majors that are inherently strong in themselves.

Yet I also see ways in which this renewal can enhance and strengthen the academic experience at Hope. I sense that some students have such a strong concern for their vocations and careers that the core curriculum is something to get through, rather than an opportunity to learn more fully what it means to live in God's world. I long to see more excitement for learning, an excitement that this is what we are privileged to do because of God's purposes and grace.

I am also concerned that relatively few students regularly read a daily newspaper, a weekly news magazine, or journals of broad interest and information. A renewed sense of what it means to be a citizen not only of this country, but also of God's world, could be a great incentive for students and faculty and staff to continue to be informed and concerned for contemporary life and thought.

Closely related to this is a matter that I spoke about a few years ago in my "State of the College" address. This was for our students to have higher expectations of themselves, not so much in terms of material success or prestige, but in what they can accomplish for good in the world, and in the process find great personal fulfillment as they live in God's world as servants of Jesus Christ. Out of this might well come another Rhodes scholar from Hope, or our first Marshall or Truman scholar. More importantly, we will see scores of graduates with a high view of themselves, a noble purpose for their lives, and confidence in God and his purposes for them and for the world.

I also see this renewal as greatly enhancing the attractiveness of Hope College to outstanding prospective students. Enrollment will certainly be a pressing issue in the next few years. A vital, dynamic, creative learning environment, that promotes wholeness of life and the enduring values that are rooted in the Christian faith, will continue to be the most significant reason we can offer these prospective students for choosing Hope College.

Community and Residential

Another of the great assets at Hope is the personal interest and concern of faculty members for their students. Almost without exception, graduating seniors speak with great appreciation of the friendship and encouragement and counsel they have received from faculty members. Such relationships, and the corresponding relationships among students, are the strengths of community life at Hope.

Yet I do have concerns about our life as a community that I believe this renewal of spirit can help us address. There are students at Hope who feel lonely and isolated. We have had only limited success in integrating minority and foreign students into the total life of the campus, and the number of these students is less than we can effectively serve. There is too much damage to physical property, including the library resources, some of which results from carelessness and some from deliberate acts. The incidents of excessive drinking are far greater than one would expect from a college that takes seriously the lordship of Jesus Christ. Each of these are areas that must be addressed as we strive for this new level of excellence, and each is best addressed in the spirit I have described above.

This spirit of renewal must touch every facet of our residential life, including sororities and fraternities. In earlier years many faculty members served as head residents in the residence halls, and this contributed greatly to the academic perspective and environment of the residence halls. This past year, for the first time in several years, a faculty couple served as head residents, with very positive results. Their leadership was one of spirit, and embraced many of the qualities referred to above.

Over the years our fraternities, which evolved from the concept of literary societies, have been a positive factor in the lives of students. At this time, however, they face a special challenge. The concept of the literary meeting, which was a central feature of fraternity life in earlier years, has largely been lost. In early years the head resident of a fraternity house also served as an advisor to the fraternity. This concept was dropped some years ago. The very physical arrangement of the fraternities tends to promote behavior that is not conducive to our goals for residential life. These problems, too, must be approached in this spirit of renewal.

Cultural

As I evaluate the cultural life at Hope, I conclude that in this area, too, we have many strengths. But I also perceive a number of ways in which the cultural life can be substantially improved, both in participation as a musician or artist or actor, and also in attending and enjoying cultural activities and events.

Such increased participation is not easy to achieve in an environment where academic pressures are high. Many students must work to procure the needed finances and we also have an emphasis on physical fitness, athletics, and spiritual matters. But I do long to see our students grow in cultural understanding and appreciation, particularly as these offer opportunities for students to enhance their gifts and abilities and to develop a comprehensive Christian worldview. Achieving this participation will not be easy, but certainly selection of programs, scheduling, and integration of cultural activities into the academic courses are all important considerations. Helping students to see the relationship of culture to faith is also a vital factor and the humanities and fine arts departments can make important contributions. Here, too, the basic commitment and spirit are vital in accomplishing such goals.

Global Concerns

The tremendous magnitude of the problems we face in the world today are evident in far greater measure in every telecast and newscast than we often wish to be exposed to. These concerns cover the gamut of problems so well known to all of us—economic, racial, and social issues, as well as the larger problems of peace and war, nuclear armament, and overpopulation. And even if we acknowledge that there is a tendency today to excessive fear over things that have not yet happened, and may, in fact, never happen, the magnitude and severity of these problems are very real and of vital concern to every responsible institution of higher education.

How does all of this affect us as a College as we think about how to achieve this next level of excellence at Hope College? It seems to me that it impinges at three levels: As an academic community, Hope must embody the biblical principles of justice, equity, and compassion in all we do. Our own concern for the environment and for careful use of resources must be evident. We must be a community where every person is treated equitably at all times, regardless of race, cultural background, or sex. A student who has spent four years at Hope should have had a good experience of what it means to live in a community where these values and perspectives on life and persons are taken seriously.

Hope also has a major responsibility to prepare students for leadership for the future. Perhaps the most effective way that Hope can make an impact on the larger issues of the world is to prepare students for leadership roles in which they can be influential in addressing these major world problems. Such larger issues as peace and disarmament and poverty are going to be addressed and solved primarily through persons of character and integrity who are in positions of leadership in business, government, education, and the media. How great it will be if there are Dag Hammarskjölds, Mark Hatfields, Mother Teresas, and Dr. Ida Scudders coming from the ranks of Hope College graduates in the future.

We need to bring into focus mature insights and understanding of these contemporary issues. This will be accomplished through our regular academic programs as well as through symposia, guest speakers, and conferences. This effort will involve going beyond rhetoric and emotions to understanding basic issues and realistically assessing alternatives. In most cases this will not involve the College taking a specific position, but rather ensuring that thorough airing and discussion of these issues is taking place, with freedom to explore alternatives and to develop creative, realistic, and even sacrifical approaches to these pressing problems of society.

OPERATIONAL IMPACT

There are a number of more tangible and operational aspects that
must also be considered if we are to achieve this goal.

Faculty

The most significant decisions a college makes is whom it adds
to the faculty. At Hope the major criteria for selecting faculty are
dedication and ability to teach undergraduates, evidence of continued endeavor and achievement in scholarship, and identification with and commitment to the Christian faith and to the goals
of the College. Some related concerns are to achieve an appropriate balance between men and women on the faculty and the
presence on the faculty of persons from minority groups. It is imperative that we maintain the highest possible standards in our
faculty recruiting, if we are to achieve this new level of excellence.

While faculty recruiting is of highest priority, *retaining* these
well-qualified persons on Hope's faculty is of equal importance.
This will involve helping faculty members to grow academically
and professionally, and in their own sense of fulfillment and
achievement. Hope has several fine programs in this area. We
have a sound program of sabbatical leaves and faculty development. In almost every department we have good offices, laboratory facilities, and support services. We have a splendid spirit of
dedication to scholarship and to being supportive of each other in
these endeavors. The areas of concern most frequently expressed
by the faculty are the level of salaries, library facilities and resources, computer resources, and certain specialized facilities.
These are matters which we must address if we are to achieve the
quantum step we seek. Having a number of additional endowed
chairs would help significantly in providing resources for salaries
and recognition of excellence. Providing expanded library facilities and library resources will be of great significance in meeting
faculty expectations and aspirations. We must, however, be sensi-

tive to new techniques for library resources which may become available in the near future. The computer needs are being addressed at present, and we are continuing to address a number of pressing departmental needs.

I do have one concern in regard to our faculty, and this has to do with academic counseling. Outstanding academic counseling is of vital importance. Ways must be found to encourage and train our faculty to do this well, and to ensure that the faculty who do this counseling are adequately recognized and rewarded. There is always the danger that those who do this counseling poorly are excused from doing it, and those who do it well do it as an added load.

Facilities

As a result of development of campus facilities over the past twelve years, Hope now has an exceptionally fine physical plant in which to carry out its mission. The completion of the De Pree Art Center and Gallery in the summer of 1982, and the anticipated completion of the renovation and expansion of the De Witt Center during the 1982-83 academic year, will provide two very important additional facilities. This leaves two major needs: facilities for the Department of Education and expanded facilities for the library. Over the next year we will be able to assess whether the office facilities we recently provided for the economics and business administration department, along with classroom space available in the De Pree Art Center and Gallery, are adequate long-range solutions to the needs of this department. At present it appears that this will be the case.

I made the mistake, after the completion of the Dow Health and Physical Education Center, of thinking that the time had come when we were essentially done with major campus development projects. Even bearing this earlier error in mind, I do believe that after providing for the education department and the library, the pressure for further campus development will be significantly decreased, and we will be able to focus more of our efforts and resources on other matters.

There is one other matter that I believe will be important to consider in the reasonably near future, and that is to develop a master plan for landscaping the campus. We have a very beautiful campus, and there are many attractive landscaping features to it. But the present landscaping lacks coherence and there are many parts of the campus in which it can be improved. The development of an overall plan for future landscaping of the campus would pay rich dividends in the future.

Closely related to campus development is another concern, namely, the future development of the area around the campus. This is a matter which needs to be treated with considerable sensitivity. The crux of my concern is that the number of rundown houses in this area is increasing. Along with this is a considerable increase in the number of incidents of molestings of campus students, altercations between students and youths in this community, and incidents of campus thefts that have been definitely related to off-campus persons. This is a problem not unique to Hope, of course, and is related to the problems of the center-city area in many cities.

There are several encouraging factors in this regard. Many faculty members and other persons in the community have bought older homes in the center city and are renovating them, though this development is taking place primarily in the area west of College Avenue. The entire area south of the campus between the railroad tracks and College Avenue is a matter of greater concern. It is also encouraging that there are plans underway to renovate the former Rusk building as an attractive office building, and some persons from the community are taking steps to develop the area around the campus. We should cooperate fully with these individuals in every way we can. However, this whole matter might well be something the College should give greater attention and priority to in the years immediately ahead.

Finances

Achieving the level of excellence to which we aspire will require very careful and judicious use of the resources we have. To achieve this, we must be creative in our planning, diligent in establishing priorities, and rigorous in our evaluation of various needs; we must maintain a lean, effective, and efficient operation of the College. One of the hallmarks of Hope in the past has been its ability to achieve the utmost possible with the limited financial resources available to us. This must be a continuing commitment as we strive for new levels of excellence.

It is also true, however, that we will need substantial additional resources to achieve our goals. One of the pressing issues we face concerns the level of charges for tuition, room, and board in the years ahead. When the level of excellence that Hope offers and the current charges we make are compared with other institutions, Hope already offers excellent value. And if we achieve a new level of excellence, we could well argue that students would be and should be willing to pay more.

At the same time we must bear in mind that Hope has always served and continues to serve many students from middle income families, and that many of these students are already finding it difficult to obtain the resources needed to attend Hope. Each year there are excellent prospective students who choose not to attend Hope because of the costs that they would have to bear personally. In most cases, these students choose a government-operated institution where the public pays the major cost of education, or a private institution that has the resources to provide greater financial aid than Hope is able to do.

What should our response be to this concern and the overall need for additional resources as we strive for a new level of excellence? We need to bear in mind the reality that we will never have resources to meet every need or to avoid having to make hard choices. But I would submit that most of the resources needed to achieve this new level of excellence could be reached if each year we had available $600,000 additional for operating expense, and $800,000 additional for financial aid. These additional funds for financial aid would be of great help in enabling us to maintain our present level of enrollment, which is also essential to the future financial well-being of the College.

How can we obtain this additional $1,400,000 needed each year to achieve this new level of excellence? If Hope could, in the next few years, add $10,000,000 to its endowment, this would provide $800,000 annually (at our present level of endowment income). This, in turn, would provide 1,000 students an average increase of $800 in their financial aid. This increase would be very significant in maintaining our present level of enrollment. A modest increase in tuition of $200 would net the College $300,000 to $400,000 in additional revenue. And if we could increase the level of Annual Fund giving by $400,000, we would have achieved our overall goal of raising an additional $1,400,000.

There are, of course, alternative scenarios by which this goal could be reached, but the scenario described above can provide a basis for thinking about this matter.

Of course we must also bear in mind that we need to raise some $5,000,000 to complete the current program of campus development referred to above, and this is the focus of many of our present efforts.

Residential Life

There are two facets to maintaining the excellence of residential life at Hope—the actual living environment itself, which I have already addressed, and the quality of the facilities themselves. In the past few years we have made significant progress in the quality of our residential facilities. The recent renovations of Van Vleck and Voorhees have demonstrated the potential of having residence halls that are conducive to both good studying and good living. The proposed renovation of Durfee offers the potential of making this the outstanding residence hall for men. The new apartment residence hall will provide juniors and seniors with an attractive alternative to off-campus living. With the art department moving out of the basement of Phelps, and international education moving out of the basement of Kollen, we will have the opportunity to provide fine study areas in these two residence halls.

There are two areas in our residential system which we need to give closer attention. Dykstra Hall is used almost exclusively as a residence hall for freshman women. In the past few years, we have had exceptionally fine leadership from this residence hall staff, and Dykstra Hall has provided a good living experience for these students. But the basic design of this hall and certain deficiencies in the construction make this a less than optimal place for students. The challenge before us is to develop a plan to offset these deficiencies and make Dykstra Hall comparable in basic facilities to the rest of our residence halls.

The second area of concern is the fraternity complex. These are basically well designed, attractive facilities. However, there are two problems. The first is that the fraternities have not been able to fill these residence halls, each of which houses forty-four students, with their own members. As a result, each of the fraternity houses is used to house a mixture of fraternity members and non-fraternity members. However, the relatively spacious basement rooms continue to be under the control of the fraternities, though in some cases non-fraternity residents are given limited use of them.

Another problem in regard to the fraternity complex is that the fraternity members have demonstrated a consistent pattern of abuse of these facilities. As a result they are clearly in the poorest shape of any of our residence halls. Further, there is little incentive for the College to provide the necessary renovation, since there is no assurance that the fraternities would give them better care in the future than they have in the past.

All of these issues will be important to address as we move forward in the years immediately ahead.

Admissions

Without a doubt, one of the most important factors in achieving this next level of excellence is to maintain our enrollment at its present level with well-qualified students. On the one hand, it seems that this should not be a problem, given the recognized excellence of Hope, the level of our charges to students, and the fact that many excellent colleges and universities are still turning away students. On the other hand, there is the reality of demographics, which indicate a substantial decline in the number of high school graduates in the years ahead, particularly in those areas from which Hope has traditionally drawn students. Coupled with this is the decline in federal and state funding for financial aid, which makes it more difficult for students to attend independent colleges.

What is to be our response? There are clearly enough well-qualified students who are interested in attending a college such as Hope, to maintain enrollment at its present level. The challenge before us is to market the College effectively and to provide financial aid to those with demonstrated need. If we can accomplish this, we should be able to achieve this important goal of maintaining enrollment at its present level with well-qualified students.

There is one additional matter relative to admissions that warrants careful study, that is, providing continuing education for this community. As the only institution of higher education in this area, Hope has both the responsibility and opportunity to meet these needs. Much of the demand for community education relates to technical subjects, such as accounting, computers, and engineering, and our faculty resources to meet these demands are very limited. However, we should carefully assess both the demands and our resources and take steps to ensure that the College is doing its best to meet this community need.

There is one other approach to continuing education that offers intriguing possibilities, and this would be for Hope to offer the master of arts degree, a terminal liberal arts degree primarily for those who wish to broaden their knowledge in the liberal arts. There is no doubt that such a program would be personally rewarding to all those who pursue it. But the program would also offer significant "professional" benefits to those who aspire to or are already involved in leadership and managerial responsibilities. This possibility would seem to be a matter that is worthy of careful exploration in the future.

SPECIFIC STEPS

What specific steps should we take at this time to move deliberately forward to achieve this next level of excellence?

Enhance and Strengthen Marketing

This marketing function involves admissions, college relations, and development. It involves informing our constituencies, the public, and the various media about the strengths and excellence of the College; it involves sensitizing all of us about the importance of effectively marketing the College; it involves getting the word about Hope College to high school students and their parents, prospective transfer students, and high school counselors. Marketing will be one of the most important activities we can undertake at this time and we must proceed deliberately to meet this need. It is also significant to note the symbiotic relationship between marketing the College and achieving this new level of excellence. Marketing the College effectively will help us achieve this goal, and achieving this new level of excellence will make it easier to market the College to prospective students and donors.

Develop Strategic Planning

A plan has been drafted for an ongoing program of strategic planning. The emphasis of this program will be on planning that relates, not to the indefinite future, but to decisions that must be made on an ongoing basis. Initial steps to implement this plan will be taken this summer with a view to having it fully operational in the next academic year.

Mobilize Leadership

Clearly this new level of excellence can be achieved only by the enthusiastic support and involvement of the entire campus community. Hope College has a strong tradition of participation of the entire College community in the decision-making processes of the College. This involves first and foremost the established administrative structure of the College, including Student Congress, but it also involves the community governance system of the College. Therefore, achieving our goal requires effective mobilization of the entire College community, and this, in turn, requires effective leadership from the president, from each administrative officer, and also from department and committee chairpersons and student leaders. The goal is to have this spirit of renewal touch every faculty member, staff member, and administrator, because we operate so much by the personal commitment to the mission and goals of the College by all members of the College community.

Involve Board Leadership

The Board of Trustees has the ultimate responsibility for the College, and will play a vital role in achieving this new level of excellence. This role will involve evaluation of the vision and program I have set before you this evening. It will involve helping us in the administration to achieve this, and evaluating the specific plans and programs we bring to you to ensure that they are consistent with this goal. It will also involve helping us in the important marketing program we hope to undertake.

These then are my thoughts on taking a quantum step to a new level of excellence. We live in troubled times. The economic uncertainties are very real, but these are overshadowed by the threat and almost unthinkable consequences of nuclear war. At a still deeper level is the crisis of the human spirit, of whether we, the human race, will be able to deal responsibly and effectively with these complex issues and problems.

God has called us to Hope College for a specific mission. What is a fitting response to that call? We must dedicate ourselves to achieve this new level of excellence in the wisdom and power of God. Then we can trust that we will more effectively influence the lives of students and help prepare them to live and serve in their day to the glory of God.

Report to the Board of Trustees
May 1982

A Balancing Act

The balance between preoccupation with one's personal life and concern for global issues is often difficult to achieve. How do Hope College students achieve such a balance? In this excerpt from the President's Report, Van Wylen briefly addresses parents and students.

Reflecting on the 1981-82 academic year at Hope College, two general trends of thinking among our faculty and students are evident. On the one hand, there is a genuine concern for the complex national and global issues we face—economic recession, armed conflicts in many parts of the world, unresolved and escalating tensions in the Middle East, issues of nuclear freeze and disarmament and, ultimately, the larger issue of peace. These are matters of tremendous importance and of vital concern to our students and faculty. At the same time, each person faces the challenge of living a daily life that is personally meaningful and significant in the context of work, family relationships, the community, and the church. Many of these personal activities seem far removed, at least for the moment, from the major issues of today's world.

We are all aware of the vital need for a balance between the personal and the global perspectives. Most of us are called at one time or another—and sometimes for considerable periods—to live our personal lives in the midst of difficult circumstances. And much of our concern and energy may go to overcome personal difficulties or to fulfill personal goals. But we are also aware that if we live for ourselves, without concern for the larger issues of peace, justice, and freedom, we soon experience a shallowness and emptiness in our lives, and we miss opportunities for the fulfillment which comes from serving others.

During this year I sensed a healthy balance between these two perspectives among faculty members and students. One could readily perceive an increasing concern for global and national issues. These concerns were genuine and were expressed in thoughtful and penetrating ways in classrooms, student media, and informal conversations. At the same time, students were preparing to live responsibly and thoughtfully in their chosen careers, to take their places in contemporary society. Yet, the challenge ever remains—for us as individuals and as a College— to avoid the extremes of either living solely for self, or of becoming so absorbed or overwhelmed by these major national and global problems that we fail to make a significant contribution to ongoing life.

One of the ways in which we hope to address this challenge next year will be our annual Critical Issues Symposium. The chosen theme is world peace, and we anticipate that a realistic grappling with the issue will result from the day's events. We will address and be concerned about global issues, and we will explore how God's peace can reign in our own lives.

President's Report 1981-82
August 1982

Liberal Arts and Careers

Career questions are important to parents as well as students. Does a college such as Hope, with its emphasis on the liberal arts, adequately prepare students vocationally?

There is a question that is frequently raised when choosing a college—will it lead to a good job? The recent emphasis on stronger mathematics and science in our schools raises this issue in a new way, because the rationale for improving teaching in these fields is that we want, as a nation, to be more competitive technologically in the world market, for if we achieve this, there will be a stronger economy and more jobs. Related to the mathematics and science teaching is a new emphasis among colleges and universities on offering more "high technology" courses and laboratory experiences to students. Again, the ultimate reason for doing this is that it will improve the economy and lead to more jobs.

What are the important factors that a student should consider in this regard? And what is our perspective at Hope on these issues? Should we become a "high-tech" college? There are several observations I would make on these matters.

First, career interests and concerns on the part of students are both legitimate and of critical importance. Our careers provide not only the income by which we live, but, of even greater importance, great potential for personal development and fulfillment. At the appropriate time (which certainly varies from one student to another), students must carefully consider their careers; colleges have a unique opportunity to serve their students by providing resources to make this a meaningful, effective process. Helping our students to know themselves, and to find careers that offer fulfillment and satisfaction is of vital importance to us; the recent expansion of the staff and activities in our Office of Career

Planning and Placement reflects our commitment to do this thoroughly and effectively.

But in all of this we like to think of "careers" and not simply "jobs." A career suggests a calling, a mission, something we do to serve others or to meet a need, work that gives us personal satisfaction and which we enjoy doing. Some (relatively few, actually) choose their careers early in life and do not depart from these decisions; others find their careers only after probing, exploring, testing, and trying this and that. Choosing a career does, however, finally involve making a decision and a commitment, and acquiring certain knowledge and skills. What a marvelous place a liberal arts college is to come to know ourselves more fully, find the calling and vocation that becomes our career, and realistically prepare for it.

What about the emphasis on "high technology"? What role should Hope College play in this? Should we try to duplicate what the major research universities are doing? While the primary responsibility for teaching high technology lies with research universities, colleges such as Hope offer a distinct advantage to students who are interested in such fields. What we offer is an outstanding education in mathematics, computers, and the sciences and we do so in the context of a strong, vital emphasis on the liberal arts. There are at least three reasons why the liberal arts background is of importance.

First, we strive to educate for life as well as vocation, to educate the whole person—mind, body, and spirit. The abundance of life does not consist so much in what we do, but in who we are—our relationships, our values, our appreciation for that which is noble and true, and our dedication to serve others. We also stress the liberal arts because technology alone cannot solve the present needs of society. To address these problems involves matters of justice and mercy, of social structures and human needs, of the human spirit and human aspirations, matters which are at the heart of the liberal arts. Finally, we stress the liberal arts, even for those who have an interest in high technology, because we are eager to prepare students who can not only do high technology, but who can also judiciously lead it and make wise use of it.

This, in essence, is our perspective on high technology. But at Hope College students are preparing for careers in many other fields which offer opportunity and fulfillment—education, business, medicine, government, and ministry, to mention only a few. Thus we strive for excellence in all we do, and to have a mature, realistic perspective on career preparation. How good that we can approach this with a view to discovering and understanding something of the purposes and call of God for us and for the world.

Presidential Update
October 1983

79849

Tuition, Salaries, and Students

Tuition should be kept as low as possible and salaries should be competitive. Van Wylen explores how one can balance those needs. And he challenges the faculty with the concepts of international education and of education as hospitality.

I trust this has been a good summer for you, a time of renewal and refreshment, a time of significant accomplishment in your research and scholarly activities, and a time to be with family and friends. I hope that in our meeting today, through a spirit of renewal, dedication, and mutual support, we can set the tone for an outstanding year for each of us individually, for our students, and for us as an academic community. In this address I will comment briefly both on some matters of immediate concern and on some more general College issues.

FINANCES

At a special meeting this past June the Board of Trustees authorized the initiation of a major capital campaign. After analyzing a comprehensive feasibility study done by an outside consulting firm, the board concluded that gifts for this campaign would be payable over a three- to five-year period and that deferred gifts and bequests would also be an important part of the campaign. Within these parameters, the board established a goal of $26,000,000. Approximately half of this is designated for the library and other campus development projects and half for the endowment. This campaign will be a truly major undertaking. During the next four months we will concentrate on soliciting gifts from the trustees and gifts of $100,000 and above. I am grateful to be able to report that the total commitment to date is already $4,000,000, most of this from members of the Board of

79849

Trustees. As part of this initial campaign we will also invite faculty members and staff to participate.

I do want to issue a word of caution about this campaign. We are soliciting funds that will be coming in over the next three to five years as well as deferred gifts through estate planning. Thus, only a limited amount of funds will be available immediately and most of these will be used for the library. The real impact of our last campaign, "The Build Hope Campaign," which was initiated in 1971, was felt after the campaign was over, with the establishment of new levels of giving and a much broader base of support. The same will no doubt be true in this campaign—the major impact will be felt after three years and will have a major impact on giving to Hope in the next decade.

There are a few other matters involving the future that I would like to touch on briefly. The first concerns priorities about our budget in the next few years. Most of us who have been here for some years will agree that financially things have improved at Hope and that we have more resources than we did formerly. But it is also evident that our expectations have gone up and that the number of relatively high priority matters has increased significantly. Hugh De Pree, former president of Herman Miller and former chairman of the Board of Trustees of Hope College, once commented to me that it is more difficult to manage when things are going well than when things are tight.

I believe that there are two major financial priorities in the years immediately ahead—faculty salaries and financial aid. In regard to faculty salaries, it is not that we have done badly in salary increases in recent years. It is simply that salaries are not what they should be, either from the point of view of what it takes to live these days or in comparison with salaries at the quality institutions with which we like to compare ourselves. Within this framework, we must give high priority to increasing faculty salaries in the next two to three years and I am prepared to give leadership in this area. This goal will, however, require the cooperation and support of all of us, lest we let other priorities detract from this important objective. If we couple this priority for an increase in salaries with the best possible merit system we can devise, I believe that we can make significant progress.

The other priority is financial aid. We made a commitment this year to significantly increase the merit-based financial aid to incoming students. This increase, we believe, was a significant factor in the increased enrollment this fall. The cost of the increase was about $200,000. We must continue such financial aid to these students, as well as making similar awards to those who will be applying for admission next year. Thus, when a four-year cycle is completed, we will have increased our merit-based financial aid budget some $700,000-$800,000. In addition, we also increased the need-based financial aid rather significantly. Thus, increased funding for financial aid is, in effect, already built into our budget.

How can we provide funds for salary increases for faculty and staff and for these financial aid programs? There are five major sources for increased income:

1. Increase the endowment, which is an important element in our capital campaign.

2. Increase giving to the Annual Fund. This will be somewhat difficult to do during the capital campaign, but we will continue to give this high priority.

3. Increase tuition, which is always a difficult decision.

4. Increase miscellaneous income, such as summer conferences.

5. Increase research support.

Each of these is important and we must give careful attention to these matters. It is also imperative that we be very diligent and careful on the expenditure side of our budget. This is the overall framework in which we will be addressing these financial matters this year.

INTERNATIONAL EDUCATION

At the suggestion of the International Education Committee, we have designated this the International Year for Hope College. Next week we will have Dr. Makoto Morii, president of Meiji Gakuin University, with us. We are deeply grateful for our ties with Meiji Gakuin University, which is one of the leading Christian universities in Japan. Very few liberal arts colleges in this country are privileged to have such a close relationship with a major university abroad as we do with Meiji Gakuin University. We are eager to maintain and strengthen this relationship, and we pledge our best efforts to accomplish this with dedication and honor.

A few weeks ago I received a very handsome volume from Japan. It was sent to me by Gordon Van Wyk, a graduate of Hope College who, along with his wife Birdie, also a Hope College graduate, has served Meiji Gakuin University for the past thirty-one years. This volume is in honor of Professor and Mrs. Van Wyk. Last Sunday I took time to read the volume (at least that portion of it which is not in Japanese), and was greatly inspired by the section titled "Professor Gordon J. Van Wyk and International Education." This section of the book gives a splendid perspective on international education at Meiji Gakuin University, and indirectly on Hope College.

The purpose of the International Year at Hope College is to bring attention to and focus upon our international education programs and our commitment as a college to bring a global perspective to all that we undertake. The fact that this is our International Year was one factor that led us to make world hunger the theme for our Critical Issues Symposium next March.

The Exxon Foundation grant, which we received in order to bring a greater international emphasis throughout our curriculum, will bring added impetus to our endeavors. I commend these activities to you and ask for your support for our colleagues who will be giving leadership to the events which have been scheduled for this emphasis on international education.

EDUCATION AS HOSPITALITY

I usually close the State of the College addresses by sharing some recent insights I have gained regarding our mission and purpose. This morning I want to do this by sharing some insights I have gained from Henry Nouwen.

In passing, I want to comment on one of the serendipities of early morning jogging. Late last month I was jogging past Kollen Hall about 6:30 a.m., when a gentleman came out of Kollen ready to jog and called to me to ask which way it was to the lake. I pointed in the right direction and told him it was a distance of three miles. Perhaps unjustly sizing up his capacity as a jogger, I suggested he settle for jogging down 12th Street to Lake Macatawa. We fell into a brief conversation, and in the process he introduced himself as Henry Nouwen. We jogged a bit together, with a pleasant conversation, and the next day I was able to arrange for several of us to have lunch with him.

Meeting him prompted me to do some further reading of the books he has written. In a delightful section in *Reaching Out*, Nouwen writes how we should show hospitality to strangers. Later, he talks about teaching as a form of hospitality. I found that by substituting the word "education" for "hospitality" and the word "student" for "stranger," this was a splendid statement of one way in which we can look at our educational mission. With apologies to Henry Nouwen, here is how this section would read:

> Education means primarily the creation of free space where the student can enter and become a friend. Education is not to change students, but to offer them space where change can take place. It is not to bring men and women over to our side, but to offer freedom not disturbed by dividing lines. It is not to lead

our students into a corner where there are no alternatives left, but to open a wide spectrum of options for choice and commitment. It is not an educated intimidation with good books, good stories and good works, but the liberation of fearful hearts so that words can find roots and bear ample fruit. The paradox of education is that it wants to create emptiness, not a fearful emptiness, but a friendly emptiness where students can enter and discover themselves as created free; free to sing their own songs, speak their own languages, dance their own dances; free also to leave and follow their own vocations. Education is not a subtle invitation to adopt the lifestyle of the teacher, but the gift of a chance for the student to find his own.

I realize there are other facets to our interactions with students—tests, papers, grades, and counseling—but I do believe that this is splendid counsel, and can help us keep all of our teaching responsibilities in perspective.

I trust this will be a rewarding year for you. Our primary responsibility is to give—of ourselves, our time, our wisdom, and our knowledge. Each of us has many other responsibilities, such as family, profession, community, and church. Yet, we know that we can grow, even as we fill these responsibilities. To do this, we do need time for ourselves, for spiritual, physical, and mental renewal. I trust that day by day we will each receive wisdom and grace for all the responsibilities of teaching and scholarship with which we are confronted, and also for these times of renewal, and that in so doing each of us will have a rich sense of joy and fulfillment. This is God's provision and gift to us. May we each experience that gift in abundance, and know in a new way the presence of Christ within us and among us.

State of the College Address
August 1984

Hope College and South Africa

During 1985 and 1986 Hope College experienced considerable controversy on the question of South Africa and the College's involvement with South Africa. Van Wylen presented the following comments to serve as guidelines in the discussion.

The fact that South African issues are very much in the news these days and have, in a variety of ways, come to us as a board, has prompted me to try to think through this matter in some depth. In order to help us develop a position on South Africa and perhaps to bring us an initial step forward in this, I thought it appropriate to set forth some of my own thinking on this matter.

The basic premises that I operate from are as follows:

1. The issues in South Africa are very complex, and we want to avoid simplistic approaches to the problems there. We want to be sensitive to all the people of South Africa. Still, where we perceive that certain policies are wrong, we should not hesitate to speak out, following St. Paul's injunction to "speak the truth in love."

2. I recognize that the issues in South Africa have a long, complex history. Still, in my judgment, the principle of apartheid is inherently wrong. To deny a certain segment of a nation's population the right of citizenship (and the privileges and freedoms related to such citizenship) because of race is wrong. Moreover, the outworking of this policy in South Africa, whereby husbands and wives and parents and children are separated, the policy of assignment to homelands where the possibility of making a reasonable living is very remote, and the discrimination in regard to a whole variety of rights are wrong. The attempt to justify apartheid on theological grounds is wrong. The loss of dignity on the part of blacks is very real and a great tragedy. Thus, in a whole

variety of ways, I find the policy of apartheid fundamentally wrong.

3. I do not believe that a nation can prosper in the long run on a policy that is fundamentally wrong. There are, in my judgment, only two options open to South Africa: a basic rejection of the principle of apartheid, with a concomitant development of a plan to eliminate the problems that have developed with apartheid, or a bloody revolution that could well devastate the entire country. For the sake of all the people of South Africa—whites, coloreds, and blacks alike—and out of a concern for these people, I believe we should urge, in every appropriate way, a change in the apartheid policy in South Africa.

4. The problems of transition from the present policy to one of genuine equity are immense and should not be underestimated. The magnitude of these problems is evident thoughout Africa. The transition from colonialization to independence has been accompanied in many countries, as many Africans themselves have testified, with grab for power, the establishment of a very small minority of elite and wealthy persons, and considerable persecution and violation of human rights.

5. What one really longs for in South Africa is a rejection of the principle of apartheid and the development of long-range plans to build on the present economic, industrial, and religious strengths of the country, with the result of a society blessed with a rich measure of justice and equity. Such a long-range plan would have many components. Education would necessarily be a major area, but it would involve many other institutions in South African society. Such a policy would also take into account tribal issues, a matter that has plagued many African countries.

6. While the racial and social problems of South Africa are very real, South Africa is far from being the only country in the world with such problems. Even in the African countries that have been totally freed from colonialism, there have been tragic persecution and violence. Uganda under Idi Amin was certainly

such a tragedy. We are familiar with many instances of violation of human rights in totalitarian countries elsewhere in the world. We should avoid two extreme positions: one in which we over-look the situation in South Africa because there are comparable problems in many parts of the world, and the other in which we focus solely on the problems of South Africa and act as though South Africa is the only such situation in the world. Neither should we ignore the racial problems that remain in our own countries.

7. As a college, we ought to focus our creative abilities and thinking on how the situation in South Africa can be best addressed within South Africa to bring a long-range resolution of this problem. We want to avoid jumping on bandwagons, particu-larly those that do not incorporate solutions that deal with the complexities of the issues in South Africa. As a college, all of our academic and creative resources, as well as a commitment to the historic Christian faith, can be brought to bear in thinking through this issue.

8. There are different viewpoints in the College community. Even though there is considerable agreement on the basic prin-ciples at stake in the racial issues of South Africa, there are also differences of opinion as to our individual, church, and national roles in addressing this matter and the strategy we follow in furthering a just, equitable, and compassionate solution. We need to live with these differences, respect one another's position, and be able to discuss these matters in a spirit of mutual support.

Given all of these considerations, what can we say about our role as a college in relationship to South Africa? Here are some thoughts.

1. We must recognize all the institutions in South Africa that can be agents in achieving responsible change. Among these in-stitutions are the government, the church, the universities, busi-ness and industry, and the media. Each of them can be very influential in addressing such changes. We also need to recognize

the role which one or two dedicated, noble individuals in South Africa can have in awakening the national conscience in regard to this issue.

2. One important way for us as a college (this would also apply to a church or a nation) to be an influence for change is to keep in communication. This communication must be frank and open, with the ability to both listen and speak. As far as South Africa is concerned, such communication should be with blacks, whites, and coloreds.

3. As a Christian college, the two most important spheres in which we can communicate and bring an influence to bear are in the universities and the churches, with the former being of special significance. Universities have often been powerful forces for social change in the past, and this is certainly a possibility in South Africa. As a college, we should be aware of what is already taking place in universities in South Africa. For example the Carnegie Corporation has made grants to the law faculty at the University of Witwatersrand relative to the legal rights of blacks and coloreds in South Africa. We should consider bringing scholars from South African universities to our campus and have Hope faculty members visit South African universities, both black and white, for a sabbatical leave and thereby become familiar with the situation and opportunities for change in South African universities. We should consider bringing South African students to study at Hope, and perhaps provide a scholarship for such students. There are no doubt many possible areas for dialogue at the university level. At the same time, we should not ignore the role of churches of all denominations in South Africa, and seek to find ways to support efforts on the part of South African churches to eliminate apartheid and develop a just and equitable society.

4. Certainly the roles of our national government and of the Reformed Church in America ought to be of vital concern to us as a college. There is, no doubt, considerable difference of opinion within the College community as to what those roles should

be. Nevertheless, we must realize that we are part of this nation and of the RCA, and the role of these two institutions, vis-à-vis South Africa, should be of vital concern to us.

5. On such issues where there are considerable differences of opinion within the College community, it is of vital importance that we preserve an environment in which the right and freedom of each member of the College community to speak his or her piece is enhanced. To achieve this, the College as a whole should exercise considerable caution in taking positions, particularly as this would relate to specific courses of action.

6. As a College, we should not limit our concern for racial equity and justice to South Africa, but be sensitive to these issues in all parts of the world where these problems exist. Further, we should continue to pay particular attention to these issues in our own country. As a College itself, we want to be sure that we are fulfilling our responsibilities to ensure that blacks and other minorities have proper opportunities at Hope College.

Report to the Board of Trustees
April 1985

Academics: A Calling from God

During his career as teacher and administrator, Van Wylen was a strong supporter of Inter-Varsity. At an IVCF Faculty Retreat he challenged these teachers at Christian and public institutions with the concept of teaching as a calling from God.

This is a day for reflection on our calling, a day to stand back and take a look at what we are doing. We are together here to put our calling and our work as faculty members into perspective. More particularly, we want to look at our work from the point of view of our Christian calling and commitment.

THE IMPORTANCE OF OUR CALL

There are several reasons why it is important to see our work and position as a faculty member as a calling of God. First, academic life is very demanding; it can be almost totally absorbing in time, energy, and thought, and it robs time from family, from recreation, and from other important activities. When determining time priorities, it makes a great difference if we approach our work as a call from God, rather than as something we have chosen because of personal interest. (Although I should be quick to add that we may not use the idea of calling as an excuse to neglect our families.)

Secondly, there can be disappointments in academic life. Tenure is always an issue—we might not receive it. A promotion may not come when we expect it. We may get a rejection slip on a publication. Our research proposal may be turned down. The course we most enjoy may be canceled, or taken over by another person. Our best student may not receive admission to the graduate school we recommended. In such disappointments it is very encouraging to sense the overarching conviction that we have been called by God, and that we find our ultimate fulfillment in serving God.

Thirdly, there is a positive reason why it is good to sense that our calling is from God. It enables us to approach our work with enthusiasm, with joy, with purpose, because the work is significant and worthwhile as a call from God. This approach is very liberating—we do our very best, and leave the results to God. I hope that, as a result of our time together today, each of us will sense anew the joy and purpose and fulfillment that comes from this assurance that we have been called by God.

THE BASIS OF OUR CALL

The distinction between the secular and the sacred is no doubt important and valid in some circumstances. However, I suspect that more often such a distinction is neither valid nor wise. I think this is particularly true in regard to vocation, especially when we think of a calling to the ministry or the mission field as sacred, and other callings as secular. I suspect that if such a distinction is to be made, it would be more appropriate at the level of purpose and inward goals, rather than in the vocational area to which one is called. I would say that any vocation can be seen as a call from God.

On what basis can one consider serving as a faculty member as a call from God—and hence a sacred call? The answer lies in a Christian perspective on both creation and redemption.

First, *creation*. This is God's world. Every part, inanimate and animate, microscopic to macroscopic, is from God. As such it is worthy of our study, including study in our academic work. A right view of creation also involves a perspective on humanity endowed with special gifts—that is, we are created in the image of God, and given special responsibilities to manage and care for God's creation. To this we add the accomplishment of men and women in their cultural settings. In a certain sense the works of humanity are also the works of God. So, all is worthy of study, because it is God's work.

Secondly, *redemption.* The guilt and sin of humanity and the evil and suffering at large in the world have in many ways ruined God's creation. Sin has entered and has marred the relationship of humanity to God, to neighbor, and to creation. However, in Jesus Christ we have redemption which encompasses all of creation. And God uses us to bring the reconciling work of Christ to bear on a fallen world.

THE NATURE OF OUR CALL

To what are we called when we are called to an academic career? This call of God involves several dimensions. At the personal level we experience a call to faith in God and faith in Jesus Christ. We strive for a living relationship with Jesus, to know Christ as Savior and Lord, and to experience the Holy Spirit in our lives. We also experience a call to be the persons God intends for us to be. Such personal dedication includes obedience, discipline, a call to holiness, a call to be Christlike. A call to healthy, wholesome relationships is involved as well. This working at healthy relationships will, for some, include spouse and other family members. For all of us it will include the church and the wider Christian community. Our vocational call (as Christians) comes to us in the context of other commitments, not in competition with them, but integrated with and complementing them.

The nature of one's call depends somewhat on the vocational field. An academic career in surgery would be quite different in terms of duty and responsibilities from a career in the classics. It also makes a difference if one teaches graduates or undergraduates, in a liberal arts or in a vocational school. However, there are some features which are common to all academicians, and these include teaching, scholarship, and being a member of an academic community.

We must keep in mind that in teaching, what we *are* as a person is often more important than what we *do*. Nowhere is this more evident than in the classroom and in our relationship with students. Our role as models is tremendously important. Cardinal John Henry Newman says this well in his essay "What Is a University?"

> No book can convey the special spirit and delicate peculiarities of its subject with that rapidity and certainty which attend on the sympathy of mind with mind, through the eyes, the look, the accent, and the manner, in casual expressions thrown off at the moment, and the unstudied turns of familiar conversation. The general principles of any study you may learn by books at home; but the detail, the color, the tone, the air, the life which makes it live in us, you must catch all these from those in whom it already lives.

All of this suggests the vital importance of the call to be a teacher: in the Christian call this involves both what we are as a person, and our mastery of the subject.

THE RESOURCES FOR OUR CALL

Finally, we should ask, what are the resources available to us as we seek to fulfill this calling with high quality and faithful Christian living? Let me just enumerate some of these resources.

1. Devotional life. Every Christian teacher needs a systematic diet of Scripture reading and prayer. The time for devotional exercises may be hard to find, but our devotional life is crucial in nurturing our professional life.

2. Broad reading. Every faculty member must be something of a theologian and be conversant with biblical and ethical issues. Such reading and discussing of issues with other Christians will help us in constructing a biblical worldview.

3. Worship. It is imperative that we become active members of a wor-

shiping community. The worship of God and the nourishment from Word and sacraments will help us to sustain our idealism and our sense of calling.

4. Fellowship. We must seek out those of like mind for mutual encouragement and upbuilding. At times each one of us will need the support of another Christian who understands our situation; at other times each one will be able to reach out in fellowship and encouragement to a colleague who needs our upbuilding.

Thus we see that ours is a noble calling. We are in a profession which often has stresses and strains. But it is also a profession which we can experience as a call from God—a call to explore his creation, to contribute to human learning and culture, and to lead students in their explorations and learning. May God give us the grace to fulfill this calling to our fullest potential and to his glory.

IVCF Faculty Conference
April 1985

What We Owe Our Institutional Heirs

When President Van Wylen had announced his retirement and the board began the process of seeking a new president, they did not ask Van Wylen to be involved in the search process. But they did ask him for a significant contribution: a statement on the present condition and the future direction of Hope College. This major statement constituted a comprehensive survey of the life of the College, and a vision for its future.

INTRODUCTION

This report has been prepared for the Board of Trustees as a preparatory step to initiating the process of selecting a new president. In many respects it is descriptive of what Hope is at present, with an emphasis on identification of our present strengths. It is also, however, a statement of what I aspire for Hope to be in the future and what I believe can actually be achieved. A number of areas of concern are identified that must be addressed if Hope is to achieve the greatness for which we all aspire, and I propose a number of suggestions how these matters can be addressed.

In an effort to gain significant input from other members of the College community in the preparation of this report, a Planning Retreat was held July 16-18, 1985. Each person attending the retreat participated in the preparation of a paper that provided the starting point for discussion on one aspect of college life. A significant number of points in this paper reflect ideas or observations presented in these papers or the ensuing discussions, and most of these reflect broad consensus reached by this group. I acknowledge with deep appreciation that many persons, including those at the retreat, have contributed to the observations and ideas in this paper.

In preparing this paper on the future of an institution as dynamic and complex as Hope College, I decided to follow the suggestions of one of the participants and selected the theme "What Do We Owe Our Institutional Heirs?" One advantage of this theme is that it clearly focuses on the future, which is the basic purpose of this paper. It also has a note of obligation which is consistent with our recognition of the fact that the decisions we make now will determine in significant ways what Hope College will be in the future. And this theme links the present with the future, because it focuses on our present responsibilities and the actions we must take now to make Hope a stronger and better recognized college in the future.

I.
THE MISSION OF HOPE COLLEGE

Those who know higher education well often stress the fact that the colleges that are doing the best and will survive with strength in the future are those that have a well-defined and well-accepted mission. Having a well-defined and well-accepted mission provides focus and direction for all the activities the college undertakes, as well as a clear basis for soliciting funds, setting priorities, and allocating resources.

Some years ago, Hugh De Pree, who was chairman of the Board of Trustees at that time, challenged me to write the mission of Hope College in a single sentence. He felt this would be a good exercise for me and that if such a statement could be developed, it would be very helpful in keeping the mission of the College before the entire College community and our constituencies. I worked on this statement off and on over a period of six to eight months and finally came up with the statement below. While this has never been formally adopted by either the faculty or the Board of Trustees, it has become widely accepted and extensively used. In the following paragraphs, certain aspects of this statement are delineated in further detail.

The mission statement I developed is as follows:

> The mission of Hope College is to offer, with recognized excellence, academic programs in liberal arts, in the setting of an undergraduate, residential co-educational college and in the context of the Christian faith.

Although *excellence* tends to be an overworked word, it is basically a useful term. In essence, it means superior performance. In attending a concert, we sense when a composition has been performed well and we describe it as an excellent performance; the concert was true to what the composer had in mind when he wrote the music. Our goal of excellence applies to everything we do academically. It also applies to values. Excellence applies to the quality of our lives, such as excellence of character and relationships, and to our life together as a community.

The term *recognized* was added for two reasons. First, it is very easy for each of us individually, and also for us corporately, to have an inflated view of the quality of our work and the significance and importance of it. The best antidote is to do superior work and in gracious ways let this be known, and then leave the judgment of whether we have truly achieved excellence to others. This is one sense in which we strive for recognized excellence.

The second reason is that it is important for our graduates that the quality of Hope be known, since this can have considerable impact on the caliber of the graduate and professional schools to which our students gain admission. This consideration is also important to those students who plan to take employment immediately after graduation, whether in business, education, nursing, or any other career. Thus, the important issue is not what *our* assessment of our quality is, but how others assess us. If Hope is known and recognized for its excellence, this will certainly help our graduates.

This fact demands that we seek to build a good public image of Hope. To achieve this the Board of Trustees, faculty, and staff must work together to build the strongest possible college we can; we must be convinced that genuine excellence is here. We then need to tell the Hope story as accurately as we can, as we get the word out to those who should know the essential nature of Hope and the qualities of our graduates and faculty.

There is general agreement on the concept of *liberal education*. We all think of a certain kind of curriculum and of typical liberal arts colleges. But there are two additional observations which need to be made about liberal education. Calvin D. Linton has observed that a liberally educated person should also be a good person:

> . . . balanced, rational, and righteous, a student and lover of virtue. And here our contemporary vision has tragically faded. Few would maintain today that our liberal arts colleges, by and large, strive above all else to inculcate virtue. Materialism, determinism, and the quantification of all knowledge makes such an attempt seem almost anti-intellectual. Today we tend to call educated that man or woman who knows much, whether it be about nuclear physics, Slavonic philology, genetics, or comparative government. We do not ask: Has his education made him wise and happy? virtuous and enlarged in his essentially human capabilities? righteous and loving? And yet these are the questions to which a liberal education is supposed to provide at least a partially affirmative answer.

Thus, the first question in regard to our education should not be, "What can I do with my education?" but, "What has my education done to me?"

The second observation involves the relationship between the liberal arts and vocation. We affirm that the liberal arts are excellent preparation for both life and vocation, and that with this balanced emphasis students can prepare to live in a world of change, assume leadership, and become a positive force in furthering noble values in a just and caring society.

We do, of course, offer majors that are definitely related to vocation and careers, including several that are in essence professional. However, in every case, these are closely related to the liberal arts, and we seek to make the liberal arts challenging, demanding, and current. We also recognize that developing a proper understanding of and appreciation for work is as important as specific vocational preparation, a perspective that can appropriately be included in the liberal arts.

One of our special strengths is certainly that we focus all of our energies on *undergraduates*. Undergraduates are capable of achieving far more than we often expect from them, and we may need to raise our expectations of our students.

The concept of a *residential* college embraces far more than having residence halls. It involves having students spend essentially their full time on campus, which provides many opportunities for out-of-classroom learning and growing experiences. It is imperative that we make the most of residential life as we seek to achieve our goals.

The concept of a residential college also embraces the idea that we are, in a very real sense, a community that includes faculty, staff, and students. This is, of course, reflected in our community governance system. But a more profound approach involves thinking of ourselves as a "covenant community." In a covenant community there are shared goals and ideals; we can seriously ask what we owe each other as teacher and student, as faculty member and administrator, as staff member and trustee. In a covenant community each person is important, each role is respected, and the concept of servant leadership is the norm.

Hope has been a *coeducational* institution since Sarah G. Alcott and Frances C. Phelps enrolled in 1878. The construction of Voorhees Hall in 1906 as the first women's residence provided an environment that led to a significant increase in the enrollment of women at Hope. Today women enroll in all the majors offered at Hope and women occupy a number of strategic teaching and administrative positions. Even so, we recognize that our commitment to be fully coeducational throughout the College requires continued diligent efforts if this goal is to be achieved.

Finally, a few comments on the phrase, *in the context of the Christian faith.* Christians in higher education frequently speak of "the integration of faith and knowledge." There is certainly merit in this concept, and we strongly affirm the importance of relating faith and knowledge. However, my concern with using this term is the danger of thinking that when we have integrated faith and knowledge, we will have "Christian psychology" or "the Christian view of history." I believe that the relationship between faith and knowledge is dynamic and ever-growing and must always be responsive to new knowledge and insights. The term "in the context of" is in my judgment a more open-ended term, which certainly affirms the Christian faith, but leaves open to continued exploration its implication for all areas of learning. It also suggests that insights gained in the academic arena can help in our understanding of faith and its meaning for life, and that we must always be prepared to evaluate academic knowledge and understanding in the light of the Christian faith.

It would be good if the term "Christian faith" could stand by itself, without a qualifier, and convey a commonly accepted meaning. But, this is not the case. And so we use a variety of adjectives—evangelical, liberal, biblical, ecumenical, conservative. If one must use an adjective, I prefer to use *historic.* This suggests that we identify with the historic affirmations of the church, which are rooted in the Bible and summarized in the Apostles' Creed. It also suggests that we focus on the basic tenets of the faith and not the details. Finally, it suggests that we are not denominational in our emphasis nor sectarian or parochial in our approach, but rather that we identify with the church as it has developed through the centuries. The fact that we are affiliated with the Reformed Church in America is certainly going to suggest that Reformed thinking will play an important role at Hope. However, by using the term *historic,* we affirm that this will certainly not be an exclusive approach.

Further, I believe that "Christian" makes a much better noun than adjective. To be a Christian has a reasonably clear meaning. It involves convictions about God in a biblical and trinitarian sense, it involves faith in God, and it involves an experience and relationship with God through Jesus Christ. But considerable variations are clearly evident in the ways in which Christians work out this faith. Thus, while certain patterns of living and practice are clearly taught in the Bible and accepted by Christians, it is very difficult, if not impossible, to clearly and unambiguously say that a given set of behaviors, ideas, or concepts is *the* Christian approach or way. Thus, if we do want to speak about Hope as a Christian college, it might be best to think of such a college as embracing a community of Christians who are seeking to fulfill an educational mission while taking seriously their individual and corporate callings as Christians. Such a community can welcome all persons, including seekers and those on the way to faith, who wish to be a part of its mission.

From this it follows that the key to maintaining the Christian character of the College lies in recruiting the right persons for the faculty and leadership positions. Dr. Robert J. Handy of Union Theological Seminary, a guest speaker at a conference of church historians held at Hope a few years ago, told how a century or so ago the trustees at Andover Theological Seminary were concerned lest the seminary become liberal and therefore drew up a rather complete doctrinal statement that all new faculty members were to agree to. Yet, fifty years later the seminary was thoroughly liberal. This suggests that to maintain the Christian character of Hope, we put our confidence in people—persons who have a meaningful intellectual and spiritual understanding of the faith and a willingness to grow and learn as the Holy Spirit works in us individually and as a community.

The Christian faith, rightly understood and applied, can provide a basis for a truly outstanding liberal arts education. It has a perspective on both time and eternity and enables us to view reality in the light of both. It provides insights on what it means to live in God's world, and incentive for discovery and development of a noble culture. It has a redemptive and incarnational perspective which gives meaning and direction and purpose to our own activities. The Christian faith can indeed be a very positive incentive for genuine excellence in liberal arts education.

As we think about Hope's mission in the future, I would especially emphasize three concerns in the mission statement: excellence, liberal arts, and the Christian faith. Hope's ability to make a significant and distinctive contribution to future generations of students rests on a determined commitment to each of these concerns. In choosing teachers and leaders for the College in the future, the ability of each person to contribute to this triad—excellence, liberal arts, and Christian faith—should be paramount. Thus the vital issue in regard to the College and its future is not only to sustain, clarify, and refine our understanding of this mission, but to translate this mission into action and reality.

One final comment on our mission. Students are at the heart and core of our mission. While scholarship and service are important activities, our *raison d'être* is students and a commitment to provide the finest education we can to all who enroll at Hope. The mission statement defines the nature of the education we offer. The methods to achieve this goal are quality teaching, challenging learning experiences, supportive relationships, a caring community, scholarship and research, and active involvement of students.

Any attempt to write a mission statement for an institution as complex as Hope College will certainly be incomplete in some ways. Such efforts always reflect the times in which they were written and the person(s) who wrote it. Further, a mission statement belongs to the community and is frequently best expressed orally and in actions, even though the ultimate authority of the Board of Trustees in regard to our mission is recognized. The one sentence statement and the additional commentary I have written is more descriptive than normative; it is an attempt to represent not only my perspective, but also what I believe to be a broad consensus among the Hope community.

II.
A LEGACY OF ACCOMPLISHMENTS
AND RELATIONSHIPS

Hope has a remarkable record of accomplishments over twelve decades that provides the foundation for both present activities and planning for the future. Over these years Hope has also developed many supporting relationships which have been a source of vitality and strength for the College. These accomplishments and relationships constitute a remarkable legacy of which we are the benefactors. Our task is to receive this legacy, use it in our work today, and develop and enhance it in order that we may pass on an even stronger legacy to those who follow us.

In the following paragraphs I have commented on two accomplishments in some detail—our academic achievements and the sense of community that has been developed. I have also identified three relationships of specific significance: our supporting constituencies, the Holland community, and the synergistic relationships we have with a number of organizations.

A. *The Academic Legacy*

Over the twelve decades that have passed since the College was founded, we have developed academic programs of considerable strength and we have retained a clear commitment to the liberal arts. A fine core curriculum is in place to ensure that each student receives a solid introduction to the liberal arts. Departments have given careful attention to the structure of the requirements for the various majors. Opportunities abound for outstanding off-campus and overseas educational experiences.

The program of summer grants initiated some years ago, coupled with the long-term commitment by the science faculty to be actively involved in research, has provided many opportunities and incentives for the faculty to pursue their scholarly interests. Much of this work has come to fruition in recent years with the publication of a remarkable number of books by faculty members. There is a continued high level of outside support for research, and we have achieved a fine record of published papers by faculty members and students.

Overall student achievement is high, and each year many graduates gain admission to the best graduate and professional schools in the country. Those who have taken positions in business, industry, government, and education after graduation do well. We receive many favorable comments on the personal qualities and abilities of our graduates.

In all of these academic pursuits a commitment to excellence has permeated our thinking. We believe that we are an outstanding academic institution, we are grateful that we are so recognized, and we are committed to becoming stronger and gaining greater recognition in the future.

This is not to say that we have no concerns at present. There is unevenness in the quality of departments and programs as well as in the various support departments and activities. There is considerable diversity in abilities, commitment to high academic achievement, and self-discipline among our students. Concerns have been expressed as to whether our best students are adequately encouraged and challenged and whether there is need for an honors program. (Seven decades have passed since a Hope graduate was appointed a Rhodes scholar.)

The academic enterprise at Hope will need careful and diligent attention in the years immediately ahead. Every person associated with this endeavor must have a vital concern for quality and ongoing self-renewal. Though the president, provost, and academic deans must necessarily provide leadership, the most important work will be done at the department level, with leadership from the department chairperson and the involvement of each faculty member of the department. For departments in which the academic programs need to be strengthened, this poses a special opportunity and challenge. Those departments in which high academic achievement is present must recognize the importance of determined efforts to retain this excellence. It is of vital importance to maintain a dedication to excellence, the willingness to devote time and energy needed to achieve this, and a spirit whereby we are willing to face reality and evaluate what we are doing, and to innovate and change as necessary.

In this regard, the periodic departmental self study and review that has been initiated presents a special opportunity for careful review, evaluation, and renewed efforts to achieve excellence. A suggestion made at the Planning Retreat may warrant further consideration—that is, to have each member of the department faculty formulate personal plans for the next few years, at the time of the departmental review. These plans would then be evaluated by the department, integrated into the departmental plans for the future, and plans formulated to provide the necessary support for each faculty member.

Maintaining a vigorous program of support for faculty development and support for research will also be of crucial importance in maintaining the quality of the academic program. We recognize that external support is vital for these activities and that faculty members play a key role in obtaining such support. It will be important for the College to support and appropriately reward such endeavors and for persons and resources to be available to assist faculty members who are seeking external financial support for scholarly activities and research.

An important matter that has been under discussion for some time is how to achieve better integration of the curriculum, particularly in regard to the core curriculum. The recent program to develop paired courses is a significant step in addressing this issue. Other possibilities certainly exist and we should carefully explore these. There is considerable national interest in this issue; the possibility of becoming a national leader in such curricular development should be kept in mind as we address these issues.

We must also pay careful attention to the balance between the liberal arts and vocational concerns of students. New linkages between the humanities departments and vocationally oriented programs offer interesting possibilities and should be carefully explored. The business program offers special opportunities. It is gratifying to see some people in the business world looking for liberally educated students. We must promote that viewpoint, because liberal education is a sound basis for making responsible business decisions. Hope's commitment to the liberal arts should be viewed as an asset in developing perspectives and programs that are responsive to the career interests of students, and in preparing students to live responsibly and assume leadership in a changing world.

At the same time, the College must be sensitive and responsive to changing interests and expectations of students. It is relatively easy for our faculty in such fields as biology, chemistry, and physics to keep up with new developments and discoveries in these fields. But in such areas as computers, electronic networking and communications, and other technological developments in which we do not have major teaching and research programs, this is more difficult. Yet, we know that many potential students have interests in these fields and plan careers in these areas. The challenge to us is to be sensitive and responsive to these interests while maintaining our strong commitment to the liberal arts and helping students integrate their vocational interests with the liberal arts.

The College should also undertake a careful study of its programs for outstanding students. We should evaluate the present policy of waiving courses on the basis of ACT scores, for in some cases it appears that this approach does not serve students well. We should also evaluate the emphasis we place on graduate studies. While admission of our graduates who apply for graduate school remains high, the percentage of our graduates who apply for doctoral programs appears to have dropped. This trend is reflected in data from recent studies which indicate a drop in the percentage of our graduates who receive Ph.D.'s or enter medical schools. One reason for this is that Hope has increased in size, and a larger percentage of our graduates are enrolling in programs such as education, business administration, and social work, where graduates normally do not pursue doctorates. However, this issue warrants our concern, and we must gather and study relevant data. Then the future course of the College in this matter should be carefully charted and we should study the possibility of introducing an honors program. It is imperative that Hope serve its superior students well. Only if we do this can we attract increasing numbers of these students to Hope.

One related matter that we will study and evaluate in the near future is advising. This will be an important study and should be done carefully and thoroughly. We should give consideration to changing our statement of faculty duties from teaching, scholarship, and service (which is usually taken to include advising) to teaching and advising, scholarship, and service, and thereby link advising to our academic pursuits, where it properly belongs, and make this a responsibility of every faculty member.

It is absolutely essential that maintaining quality in our academic programs be a matter of highest priority. This is not only an essential element of our basic mission, but our future as a college depends on achieving this. While the emphasis on the personal dimension that is present at Hope, the advantages of the small college and personal development, and our commitment to the Christian faith are factors that will continue to attract students to Hope, genuine excellence will always be of vital importance. To this we must continue to give top priority.

B. Hope—A Residential, Academic, and Covenant Community

One of the strengths that Hope has developed over the years is a sense of community. Many visitors to the campus comment on this and most of our faculty and staff not only sense this and are grateful for it, but work hard to retain and enhance it.

There are three perspectives from which the community at Hope can be viewed—a residential community, an academic community, and a covenant community. These are, of course, closely related and in many ways overlapping, but I will discuss each one separately.

1. A Residential Community

In a very real sense, Hope is a residential community. The most tangible evidence is our residential system for students, which currently involves 1,675 students living on campus and 1,750 students taking meals on campus.

Our residential system has several strengths. We have good facilities with a diversity of housing arrangements, including single rooms, double rooms, apartments, and cottages; an established arrangement for leadership from head residents and resident assistants; good maintenance and periodic renovation of residence halls; and a reasonable effort toward residence hall programming. The increased number of faculty members who are serving as head residents has been a positive factor. Western Food Service does an excellent job of providing quality, attractive meals. The custodian-maintenance staffs not only give fine care to the facilities, but often provide encouragement and support to students. The residential system provides an environment which has contributed much to the growth and development of many students. The effective work of the Health Clinic and Counseling Center is recognized and appreciated by the community. There are many opportunities for student involvement and personal growth through a wide range of religious, social, cultural, academic, and athletic activities.

There are, however, concerns about the residential life at Hope. Residence halls do not consistently provide an environment that is conducive to academic achievement and personal growth. At times there is less respect and concern for others and less care for the physical facilities than one would expect in the kind of community we aspire to be. Changing cultural and social norms present special challenges in maintaining a quality residential system. These problems have been compounded in recent years, because of lack of residence hall spaces, with the result that a significant number of sophomores and juniors, as well as seniors, have been granted permission to live off campus. This detracts significantly from the residential character of Hope.

Concerns are frequently expressed from a variety of perspectives about the fraternities and sororities. In the past these organizations have played a positive and significant role in the education and development of students. While improvement in pledging has been made in recent years, many faculty members feel that these activities still detract significantly from academic achievement at a critical time during a student's freshman year.

Concern is also expressed that some aspects of the pledging process have been dehumanizing and counterproductive to developing maturity, responsibility, and high academic achievement. An increasing number of fraternities and sororities are moving into cottages, but it is not clear that well-defined and carefully evaluated procedures and objectives have been established for these moves. All of this is not to say that there are not substantial potential benefits to members of the fraternities and sororities and to the College as a whole. Rather, it appears that many of the potential benefits that fraternities and sororities offer are not being achieved at present. Thus, the question becomes: How can we gain the full potential of residential life?

A first priority is to develop a clear, well-accepted purpose for our residence halls. I recommend that we require all freshman, sophomore, and junior students to live on campus, unless they are married or are bona fide commuter students, with senior students having the option to live on campus. This decision would require construction of some additional residence halls. Careful attention must be given to the design of these residence halls, to ensure that the room arrangements, size of facilities, and overall ambience will further the goals for the residence halls and for the College.

The most important dimension of our residence halls is the maintenance of an environment which is conducive to scholarship, learning, and personal development. The key to this is leadership from the residence hall staff and from students. A sense of partnership between the staff and students can be a key factor in enhancing the quality of life in our residence halls, though the leadership to achieve this must necessarily come from the residence hall staff. We must also provide quality programming in the residence halls. We should continue to encourage faculty members and their spouses who feel called and qualified to serve as head residents, to apply for such positions.

We must carefully review the matter of living arrangements for fraternities and sororities, with all of its implications for the total community. This is important not only for the benefit of the members of fraternities and sororities, but also for the entire College community. It is important that we address this issue now, because of the long-range planning for campus facilities.

Further, at an appropriate time in the near future, a definitive study of fraternities and sororities at Hope should be undertaken. All segments of the community, including fraternities and sororities, should be involved in this study, which should focus on the goals of these organizations, an evaluation of how these goals relate to the mission of the College, and methods to achieve these goals.

2. An Academic Community

Hope is above all an academic community in which faculty, students, and staff are partners in teaching, learning, and scholarship. This perspective of our community is readily broadened to embrace the range of cultural activities, intercollegiate athletics, and other events that involve participation by many members of the College.

As an academic community Hope has many strengths. Perhaps the most significant is the quality and strength of the relationship between faculty members and students. The commitment of faculty members to be outstanding teachers, not only in the classroom but also through their personal interest in their students, their willingness to go the second mile to assist students, their interest in having students as friends, is certainly one of the major strengths of the College. For this the community owes a debt of gratitude to members of the faculty.

My greatest concern in regard to our being an outstanding academic community is that I long to have a greater love for and commitment to learning and scholarship permeate the campus. Such a spirit is present in measure already, but I do not believe we have reached our full potential. These attitudes should not be evident only in formal courses and our regular curriculum, but in our conversations and discussions, in our extracurricular activities, and as we establish priorities in the use of our time and resources. This spirit cannot be programmed. Rather, it must be instilled through a variety of academic, cultural, and religious activities and through the lives and actions of our faculty and staff. Certainly the new library will offer a major opportunity to promote scholarship and learning, simply because of the availability and attractiveness of this facility.

3. A Covenant Community

Hope can also be considered a Christian community. This fact certainly contributes to making Hope a place in which care and support for one another is present, where leadership is seen from the perspective of being a servant, and the recognition that before God we are all equal. However, because the term "Christian community" is used in many different contexts, it is not a very precise term.

I believe that "covenant community" is a better term and has particular relevance for Hope. The basis of this covenant concept is the biblical idea of meaningful, caring, personal relationships. Our relationship with God through Christ is the basic covenantal relationship. But this idea is readily extended to our relationships with each other as we work together at Hope to achieve our mission. The commitment of all departments of the campus to this mission forms the basis for a unique and special kind of community.

Three things stand out in my understanding of this idea. The first is that this community recognizes that each person has been made in the image of God and has inherent worth, significance, and dignity. Further, though there is a diversity of roles within the community, with students, faculty members, the Board of Trustees, and administrators having their duties and responsibilities, we are all equal before God and we are called to live in meaningful, supportive relationships with each other.

Secondly, in a covenant community there is respect for the needs of each individual as a person, and the College makes bona fide efforts to meet these needs. These efforts include opportunities to be involved and thereby fulfill one's responsibilities and to exercise one's gifts; opportunities for growth and personal development; space to become what one can be; and support and love from other members of the community. Thus, in a covenant community there is a strong emphasis on the individual, and on the responsibility of the community to meet personal needs. There is, of course, also the responsibility of each individual to the community, which makes this a two-way relationship.

Thirdly, interpersonal relationships are a vital dimension of a covenant community, and it is in this regard that the concept of a covenant is especially significant. A covenantal relationship is different from a contractual relationship. While a contract is important in specifying and clarifying certain matters, it does not provide the basis for meaningful relationships, for resolving conflict, or for coping with change. In a covenant relationship there are shared ideals, goals, and actions. There is also a commitment to keep listening and talking when conflict arises. In such relationships there is courtesy and civility and an attempt to be sensitive and caring for each other. Some of the marks of a covenant community are a commitment to truth, to openness, to being able to discuss what we owe each other and the institution, and to servant leadership. In a covenant community there is emphasis on clarity and openness (except when confidentiality with respect to others must be preserved), on being truthful with each other, on being open to scrutiny and even on being vulnerable.

There are many ways in which Hope is already a covenant community. There is a caring spirit on campus, a high level of trust is present, and channels of communication tend to be open. This is not to say that there are not areas that need attention. More can certainly be accomplished, but we do have an excellent base from which to begin.

There is an area of major concern, however. This is the relatively small number of minority persons on the faculty and staff and of minority students who have enrolled at Hope in recent years. Throughout the College there is a commitment to recruit minority persons for the faculty and staff and to enroll larger numbers of minority students. The Admissions Office has made genuine efforts to achieve this latter goal. But the fact is that we have not achieved our goal. The result is not only significant in terms of lost opportunity to enable minority students to receive an education at Hope, but the covenant community at Hope is impoverished because of this lack of diversity among faculty and students and our failure to be more representative of contemporary society. The recent appointment of a director of Minority Student Affairs was a positive step and can provide the base on which to build in the future.

In recent years we have done well in terms of the number of students with handicapping characteristics and international students, and our ability to integrate them into the campus community. However, in these areas, also, we need continued attention to be sensitive to these persons and responsive to their aspirations and needs.

Further development of the concept of a covenant community has considerable potential to strengthen the College in the future. As we clarify this concept in our own thinking and develop strategies to achieve this goal, we can significantly enhance the overall environment of the College and make it a stimulating, challenging place in which to work and learn. In particular, if we avoid the "we-they" syndrome, which can so easily prevail in a community—faculty versus administration, students versus faculty, staff versus faculty—we will not only make Hope a more enjoyable place to work, but be more effective in accomplishing our mission. We want to pursue our goal of excellence in an environment that we find supportive, enjoyable, stimulating, and rewarding.

C. Our Supporting Constituencies

Our supporting constituencies include a number of groups that are of vital importance to the College. Among these are alumni, parents, friends, and the Reformed Church in America, including that remarkable organization, the Women's League for Hope College. These groups, and individuals in these groups, play a vital role in the life of the College in admissions, financial support, public information about Hope, and through their encouragement and prayers. It is imperative for the College to view these as relationships of mutual support, and to consistently seek ways in which we can fulfill our responsibilities to these constituencies.

In general, these relationships are healthy at the present time. This has been particularly true of our alumni. In recent years, some forty-two to forty-three percent of our alumni have contributed annually to the College, and many have served as volunteers in a variety of capacities. Class reunions have been well attended and alumni activities in a number of areas have been effective. Of special significance has been the involvement and support of recent graduates. Their loyalty and support are evident in many ways, which bodes well for the future of alumni support for the College. The Alumni Board has been particularly effective in recent years, as it has provided an important link between the alumni and the College, and has served as a vehicle for input from alumni into the affairs of the College.

While we do not have a formal parents' organization, we actively seek to involve parents of both present and former students in a variety of ways. A number of these parents have been actively involved in our admissions program.

The group we identify as "friends" includes those persons whose association with the College is neither as alumni nor parents. Many of these are members of the RCA; others are residents of the Holland area; still others are those who have become acquainted with the College and want to be a part of its mission.

One of our most important constituencies is the Reformed Church in America. Hope owes its existence to leaders in the RCA. Since the mid-1850s this affiliation with the oldest denomination in the country, which itself blends a commitment to the Reformed and historic Christian faith with a willingness and openness to work with others, has been a major source of strength to Hope. Of particular significance is the relationship with the RCA which resulted from the reorganization of the Board of Trustees in 1968. At that time the church granted title of the College to the Board of Trustees, and this board is now fully responsible for its operation. The RCA's formal involvement with the College is the election of twelve members of the Board of Trustees by the General Synod of the RCA. Of comparable significance is the "Covenant of Mutual Responsibilities," drawn up in 1969, which delineates the commitment the College and the RCA make to each other. The financial support we receive from the RCA is also very significant. It is important to recognize, however, that this support comes not from the denomination, but from individual congregations. Thus, it is imperative for the College to keep close contact with the individual congregations and their pastors.

The Women's League for Hope College is a unique organization that is superbly effective in supporting the College. This organization, which was founded in 1925, has as its primary purpose the furnishing of residence halls, so that these will be attractive places for students to live in and conducive to gracious living and personal development. Over the past sixty years this splendid organization and its thousands of active members have contributed more than $800,000 to the College. The annual Village Square, the major activity of the Women's League, continues to be an important public event for the College. Continued support, encouragement, and expressions of appreciation to the leaders and all those associated with Village Square will be important for our future relationship with this remarkable supporting organization.

These constituencies are a very special legacy of the College. Each is very significant to our future. It will be of vital importance to maintain the active, enthusiastic support of each of these groups and all the individuals involved. The financial support and the contributions these persons make to our admissions and public relations activities will be of tremendous help as the College faces difficult challenges in the future.

To achieve this goal, several areas which will need special attention can be identified. As regards our alumni, we must:

1. strive to involve all of our alumni in class reunions, alumni chapters, and activities on campus, and maintain good communication with them. Involving graduates in their early years as alumni is especially important;

2. acknowledge the accomplishments of our alumni—to them individually, and publicly as appropriate;

3. continue to work with the Alumni Board so that it has a vital, dynamic place in the life of the College;

4. review our Homecoming activities to be sure that we are responsive to all alumni.

We are not involving parents in the life of the College as well as we might. This matter should be recognized and addressed. The first step is to clarify the responsibility for parent activities, since both the Development Office and the Student Affairs Office have a stake in this. The second step is to develop a comprehensive program. More can certainly be done on Parents Weekend to recognize parents, involve them in the life of the College, and honor them. Perhaps we can develop an effective program for parents for Commencement weekend. Communication with parents should also be reviewed, and consideration given to developing a formal parents organization.

We must continue to develop and strengthen our relationship with the RCA. This is a difficult task because this must be done primarily at the level of individual congregations, which number some 900. There are special opportunities for recruiting minority students through the RCA, because the RCA has an increasing number of congregations that have large numbers of blacks, Hispanics, native Americans, or Asian members. A fresh strategy for our relationship with RCA churches should be a high priority matter.

Although our relationship with the RCA is special, we should not neglect association with other churches and denominations. Our Christian perspective is broader than the RCA and this should be reflected in our relationships and involvement with other denominations and churches.

Two general observations can be made regarding all our constituencies. The first is that good communication is essential, because for many persons this is the primary channel for receiving information about the College. These communications should relate, as accurately and sensitively as we can, the mission of the College, how this mission is being fulfilled, how our constituencies are playing a role in achieving this, and how the mission of the College is being fulfilled through our alumni. In doing so we must recognize the diversity of ages, interests, and points of views on many issues that exist among our constituencies and be sensitive to this. We would like each of these persons to feel a genuine sense of ownership in the College. This will necessarily be somewhat different from the ownership that the Board of Trustees, faculty, and students feel. Nonetheless, it is possible to develop a genuine spirit of ownership among our constituencies. This will certainly enhance the potential for financial support and for assistance in recruiting students. However, it also increases the responsibility we have to be concerned for and supportive of those persons who are part of this larger Hope College community.

The other observation is the vital importance of saying thank you—promptly and graciously—to all those who support the College in any way. This should be done not only by the spoken and written word, but also in our attitudes and actions in being good stewards of all the resources entrusted to us. Doing this is not only a delightful privilege, but does much to develop a sense of ownership and to enhance the long-term support of the College.

D. The Holland Community

Hope College enjoys excellent relationships with the Holland community. One reason for this is the fact that Hope College has been an integral part of the community since shortly after it was founded. The religious, cultural, and social life of the College and the community have been intertwined over the years and have provided the basis for mutual support. The strategic role that Hope alumni and faculty members play in the community has also been a positive factor. The size of the community and the size of the College are both such that symbiotic relationships can exist without either party being threatened. The significant impact the College has in the community is recognized and appreciated, as are the many contributions and services the city provides to the College. Students have many opportunities for involvement in the community with work experiences and volunteer activities such as Higher Horizons and internships. Certainly the Holland community is a very important resource for the College. The College, in turn, contributes much to the economic, cultural, social, and spiritual life of the community.

As we look to the future, three areas of opportunity can be readily identified in which the College and the city must work closely together. The first relates to the downtown area. Clearly, a healthy, attractive downtown is a great asset to the College. The College, in turn, does much to support a healthy downtown, both by maintaining a safe, pleasant, well-kept area adjacent to the downtown and through the faculty, staff, students, and visitors who shop in the downtown areas. The issue of shopping malls and where they should be located has been an important topic in our community recently, and certainly has implications for the College. It is clearly evident that the College should be active in working with the city and various agencies within the city relative to the downtown area.

A second area of importance relative to the city is the area surrounding the campus, particularly to the north, east, and south. The homes and buildings in these areas are aging and in some cases deteriorating. These areas certainly have the potential to become a negative factor on both the College and the community. The College should give careful attention to this and work closely with the city in developing responsible solutions.

E. Synergistic Relationships

Hope participates in a number of organizations and has relationships with a number of others, all of which can be described as synergistic. Those organizations in which Hope participates include the Great Lakes Colleges Association, the Michigan Intercollegiate Athletic Association, the Michigan Colleges Foundation, the Association of Independent Colleges and Universities of Michigan, the National Association of Independent Colleges and Universities, the American Council of Education, and the Institute for European Studies. It has been helpful for Hope College to be affiliated with each of these organizations and Hope, in turn, has contributed to their strength.

With other organizations Hope has also developed relationships which are mutually supportive. Included in these are Western Theological Seminary, the public and Christian school systems in this area, and organizations such as Young Life, which is now conducting its Summer Institute on the Western Seminary and Hope campuses. All of these associations are important resources for the College.

Accreditation is an important dimension in American higher education, and provides a means whereby the public can be assured of the quality of the education an institution offers. The institution-wide accrediting agency is the North Central Association of Schools and Colleges. In each recent evaluation, Hope has been accredited for ten years, the maximum period for which accreditation is granted. In addition, several specific programs have been accredited by the appropriate organizations. These include the National Council for Accreditation of Teacher Education, the American Chemical Society, the National Association of Schools of Art, the National Association of Schools of Music, and the National Association of Schools of Dance. Accreditation of the nursing program is expected in the near future.

These accreditations are important to us as a College, for these provide opportunities for us to evaluate ourselves, to be evaluated by others, and to be an integral part of the higher education community. Each year a number of faculty members participate in accreditation visits to other institutions.

Certainly Hope must continue to develop and nurture these various relationships in the future. We must, first of all, fulfill our responsibilities, including active participation in these organizations. One thing we could well do is to have a number of these organizations hold their conferences on our campus. For example, relatively few of the Great Lakes Colleges Association conferences are held at Hope. The new Maas Center will be an important resource to enable us to host such conferences. One very significant by-product of these synergistic relationships is that they provide opportunities for others to come to know Hope and thus further our efforts to enhance our national reputation.

F. The Board of Trustees

One other important legacy must be cited. This is the Board of Trustees. In 1968, the Board of Trustees was reorganized and reduced in size. At that time a deliberate effort was undertaken to bring to the board persons from a diversity of professional fields that bear on the work of the College. Persons were chosen who were not only exceptionally well-qualified in their own fields, but who had a commitment to Hope College and were concerned about its future.

The organization of the board into four standing committees (Academic Affairs and Admissions, Business and Finance, College/Church Relations and Development, and Student Life) enables each board member to participate in depth in one aspect of the work of the College. The chairman of each of the committees serves on the executive committee, which enhances the effectiveness of this committee. It is important to note, however, that the executive committee does not meet at the time the full board meets, but limits its meetings to once between board meetings. All of the actions of the executive committee are reported to and ratified by the full board. Every effort is made to keep the board fully involved, so that it can effectively fulfull all of its responsibilities in the ownership and operation of the College.

At the time the board was reorganized, it was decided that two faculty members should serve on the board. These persons are elected by the board from nominees submitted by the faculty, with two nominees submitted for each position to be filled. Having faculty members on the board has worked very well, primarily because it has been clearly understood by all that these persons are not faculty representatives to the board, but faculty members who have been elected by the board and have all the responsibilities of being a board member. It is recognized by all that the President must always be the channel of communication between the faculty and the board.

Hope's Board of Trustees functions very effectively. This is due first of all to the development of a good organization within the board and arranging meetings so that the board can be fully involved in an efficient manner and without undue expenditure of time. A far greater reason for the effectiveness of the board is the character, ability, and dedication of each board member. These women and men give very generously of their time, energy, and resources, and through their service on the board, the College has been greatly strengthened.

Much more could be written about the accomplishments and supporting relationships of the College and the remarkable legacy this has been for those of us who are serving the College today. As we think about our institutional heirs, and the legacy we will pass on to them, we realize the vital importance of building an even stronger record of accomplishments, with a particular emphasis on quality, and developing the finest possible supporting relationships. The path ahead will not be easy for colleges and universities, and competition for resources and students will be keen. We have much going for us, but the task of building for the future will require wisdom and diligence, individually as well as in our corporate life, and in all of our external relationships.

III.
ASSETS—FINANCIAL AND PHYSICAL

What do we owe our institutional heirs in assets, both financial and in physical facilities? In addressing these issues we again affirm that none of these assets is an end in itself. Neither balancing the budget, nor increasing the endowment, nor building a new library is a goal in itself. Rather, these assets are simply resources we need to accomplish our mission. However, because these are necessary and essential, they play a prominent part in our thinking and much time and energy is devoted to securing and managing these assets. But we must never think that having these assets in abundance will in itself ensure that our mission will be achieved. The challenge will always be to be grateful for the assets we have and to use them wisely and carefully.

A. Finances

Certainly we owe our heirs an institution that is healthy financially. This financial health involves maintaining good accounting, auditing, and record systems, a reputation as a responsible institution to do business with, adequate financial reserves to enable the College to weather lean periods, a strong development program, and equitable and competitive compensation programs.

Hope College, though it is certainly not a wealthy institution, is basically in good financial condition. At the close of the last fiscal year the market value of the endowment was $14,500,000; the book value of the physical plant was $46,500,000; and total indebtedness was about $8 million with half of this being in long-term, low-interest government loans and the balance in fairly low-interest, tax-exempt bonds. The College has operated with a balanced budget each year for the past eighteen years. For the past four years, gifts to the College have totaled $5 million to $7 million annually. The Campaign for Hope, which has a goal of $26 million, has to date raised $19 million in gifts, pledges, and deferred gifts.

However, there are certain concerns. With an annual operating budget of $24 million, the College has reserves that are only minimally adequate. We are very dependent upon tuition for income—approximately eighty percent of our operating income is from tuition and related charges. This places a great burden on us to maintain enrollment and to raise tuition annually in order to have the necessary operating funds. Further, it is imperative that we balance the budget each year. Thus, finances are a matter of concern, both in our current operations and as we build financial resources for the future.

In developing plans and strategies that will provide financial assets for our institutional heirs, the following factors should be borne in mind.

1. During the past four years the College has issued tax-exempt bonds to cover the costs of constructing and renovating certain residence halls and for computer resources. This decision was made because of our conviction that these facilities and equipment were necessary if we were to achieve our goal of excellence and maintaining stable enrollment. This has, however, added to the funds we must raise annually for debt service.

Recently the state of Michigan has authorized a tax-exempt bond issue to assist private colleges in their construction programs. Hope College has been approved for $13 million in such funds. About $1,500,000 is designated to cover prior construction projects, with the balance designated for the new library and the other projects associated with the Campaign for Hope. Our goal is to raise all of the funds for these projects through the Campaign for Hope and thus to have reserves to pay off these bonds.

Thus, these borrowed funds really become low-interest interim financing for the intended projects.

One of the important challenges will be to manage all of these funds so as to minimize interest costs, maximize income, and ensure that funds to repay these bonds are available when needed. The bonds, as well as those previously issued, must be repaid within ten years. The goal should be to have these facilities available as soon as possible, all indebtedness paid on schedule, with the College in a strong financial position in ten years.

2. Hope is a better, stronger institution than one might expect, given our financial resources and the level of charges to students. Therefore, it is quite clear that great economies are not readily available, particularly in view of our commitment to excellence. However, careful attention must continue to be given to ensure that priorities are carefully established. We must recognize that we cannot do everything. Further, a college is labor intensive; at Hope more than half the operating budget is for salaries. Very specific attention must be given to the hiring of additional persons for our faculty and staff. Over the past several years the student-faculty ratio has dropped from 15.1 to 13.6. What is of special concern is that this has not happened as a result of specific overall planning, but by responding to individual requests and needs.

3. The fact that we are heavily dependent upon enrollment leads directly to questions of the level of charges for tuition, financial aid, and the availability of family resources for College expenses. We must ensure that we do not price ourselves out of the market. Having adequate financial aid programs is also an important factor. Further, we are committed to a reasonably ambitious program of merit-based scholarships.

All of this leads to a major consideration. How can we best help families and their children cover the costs for college? Are there creative ways in which this matter can be addressed? The emphasis on loans does not seem to be an adequate answer. This is an issue which warrants careful attention in the future. The answers to these questions are not easy, but Hope could be in a leadership position if we can find creative, innovative ways to address this important matter.

4. With the increase in the endowment that has been achieved over the past decade, and the additional increase that is anticipated through the Campaign for Hope, management of the endowment will become increasingly important. The goal is to provide maximum income while being prudent to ensure preservation of capital. The Board of Trustees has special responsibility in this regard, and the recently-appointed Investment Committee should prove very helpful. Effective management of the endowment is one of the most important aspects of providing adequate assets for our institutional heirs.

5. Over the past decade a strong development program has been established. The Build Hope Campaign, a capital campaign that was initiated in 1971, provided an excellent foundation on which to build this program.

The Campaign for Hope, while very significant in itself in gaining important resources, will provide the base for developing new levels of accomplishments in our development program in the future. When the Campaign for Hope is completed, we will strive to achieve higher levels of giving for the Annual Fund and continue a vigorous program of planned giving. The Annual Fund will then provide increased funds for operating expenses, and the planned gifts will enable us to continue to build the endowment of the College.

B. Facilities

Hope has remarkably fine facilities to pass on to our institutional heirs. The building program which began in 1970 with the construction of the De Witt Center has carried forward to the present. As a result of this building program, coupled with the closing of

12th Street, we now have exceptionally fine campus facilities. Further, for the past several years there has been a consistent maintenance program, with the result that our older buildings are in excellent condition.

There remain, however, a number of campus development projects which we must undertake. When completed, they will greatly enhance the resources available to achieve the excellence to which we aspire.

1. A New Library

The working drawings for this facility have been completed. Construction is scheduled to begin in the spring of 1986 with completion in the fall of 1987. This attractive, functional building will be a very significant academic resource for decades to come and will be both symbolic and tangible evidence of our commitment to academic excellence.

2. Additional Classroom and Laboratory Space

At present there is an overall shortage of classrooms as well as a shortage of laboratory space for certain departments. The proposed connecting link between VanderWerf Hall and Van Zoeren Library will meet most of these needs. It is imperative that we do a careful analysis of the size and number of classrooms needed, so that we can optimize the use of this space.

The future use of Van Zoeren Library must be carefully developed to ensure that this is designed and utilized so as to maximize its effectiveness for the entire campus community.

3. New Residential Facilities

If Hope is to achieve the goal of having all freshman, sophomore, and junior students living on campus, as well as encouraging seniors to remain on campus, it will be necessary to construct residential spaces on campus for some 200 students. It will be particularly important to design these so that these residences are attractive to the students and conducive to serious academic work as well as personal development. This will require careful, creative planning. Particular attention should be given to increasing the number of single rooms on campus, though these must be designed so that a genuine sense of community is retained.

4. A Long-Range Plan for Campus Development

Recently, the architectural firm of Shepley, Bulfinch, Richardson, and Abbott was retained to develop a master plan for the campus. The emphasis is not on the central area of the campus, but on the peripheral areas. Such planning will be very important in delineating the boundaries of the campus, developing appropriate entrances and parking areas, and doing what we can to enhance the areas that surround the campus. Through this master plan, decisions will be made regarding the location of additional residence halls and the properties the College should acquire as they become available. A very important aspect of this planning is to develop open areas on campus.

Another very important aspect of this long-range plan is to integrate the planning of our physical facilities with the city of Holland and Western Theological Seminary. It is exciting to visualize an attractive part of the city that begins with the downtown area and then extends to Hope College, Western Theological Seminary, and other areas surrounding the downtown.

5. A Master Plan for Campus Landscape

As the various campus projects have been completed over the years, we have done some landscaping around each building. We have not, however, developed a master plan for landscaping the entire campus. As an adjunct activity to the construction of the new library, a master plan for campus landscaping should be developed. This would include consideration of location of various walkways on campus as well as plantings. The planting of trees should be a prime consideration in this master plan, particularly in view of the fact that a number of trees, including those in the pine grove, have been destroyed by disease or storms in recent years. The biology department should be involved in developing this master plan.

6. Athletic and Intramural Facilities

The Edkal J. Buys Athletic Fields are very attractive and functional; however, there are additional possibilities for these areas. It would be desirable to have a regulation softball field in this area. Also, if the area along the creek could be cleared out, it would be an attractive area for hiking and cross-country skiing. Special attention should be given to providing space for intramural athletics, both on the campus area and at the Buys Athletic Fields. In the long run, consideration should be given to constructing an indoor tennis facility near the campus.

7. Capital Equipment and Computer and Word Processing Facilities

The need for instrumentation, computer and word processing equipment, and other capital needs is very real and will always be with us. Finding the resources to procure and maintain this equipment will be a continuing challenge for both the administration and the faculty.

In the construction of all facilities the College must attend to quality, function, beauty, and economy of both construction and operation.

The financial resources and physical facilities of the College are in fine condition today. Much, however, remains to be done to build on our present strength and to provide the assets needed to fulfill our mission with excellence in the years ahead. This will continue to be a significant, exciting, and rewarding challenge.

IV.

MOMENTUM

We also owe our institutional heirs momentum—a dynamic, on-going operation that is not only achieving our mission at present, but can carry the College with vigor into the future. In the following paragraphs, a number of factors that relate to the momentum are identified and commented on. These are matters that can provide the vitality and enthusiasm needed to carry the College into the future with strength and excellence. Although momentum is of vital importance, it comes as a by-product from other factors, rather than as a primary goal.

A. Faculty and Staff Recruiting

Among the most important actions we take are decisions on whom we add to the faculty. Recruiting persons who have outstanding academic ability, the commitment and skills to be excellent teachers, an understanding and acceptance of the mission of the College, the capacity to be effective members of the community, and who meet our established policy in regard to the Christian faith must always be a matter of high priority. Further, it is essential to have a stimulating, supportive environment so that these persons can quickly become effective, productive, contributing, and enthusiastic members of the community. Opportunities must be provided for these persons to exercise their leadership gifts, though not necessarily by accepting an administrative assignment. An enthusiastic, cooperative, productive faculty is certainly an essential element in maintaining the momentum of the College.

In identifying potential faculty members, there should be a strong emphasis on networking, through which we maintain contact with individuals who know Hope and can recommend outstanding candidates. We may need from time to time to depart from our emphasis on recruiting primarily at the assistant professor level. A position as a visiting faculty member can be effective for both the prospective faculty member and the College to decide if a permanent appointment would be the right decision. We need to provide opportunities for prospective faculty members to exercise their option of deciding whether Hope is the right place for them, which, in turn, will enhance their sense of ownership if they join us. At the same time, we must put forward our best efforts to recruit those we feel would contribute much to the College. For an institution such as Hope, with a strong sense of community, the recruiting process is probably more important than the tenure process in developing an outstanding faculty.

What is true for the faculty in regard to maintaining momentum is also true in the non-academic sphere, for the support staff plays a vital role in maintaining the quality and momentum of the College. A support staff in which each individual has a sense of ownership of the College and enthusiasm for his or her work and role in the College community can contribute a great deal to the work of the College and to maintaining momentum. Opportunities for personal growth, promotion, and involvement in the campus community are important factors in maintaining enthusiasm among our non-academic staff.

B. Achieving Excellence

Few things do more to kindle enthusiasm and to maintain momentum than achieving excellence. Knowing we have done well and having our work recognized as such by others provides a sense of fulfillment that inspires enthusiasm and gives courage to attempt new levels of achievement.

Achieving excellence implies evaluation. However, making good evaluations in a college setting is seldom easy. Learning how to do effective evaluations is a matter to which we must give continued attention. A few suggestions are made here that may contribute to our discussions on these issues.

One step is certainly a willingness to be vulnerable. To listen to an evaluation and possible criticism of what we have done is never easy, even when done in the most constructive way. But a

willingness to be vulnerable is essential for learning about ourselves, which, in turn, is essential in achieving excellence. Taking
the initiative to honestly inquire about our performance is very
helpful and can provide an environment in which those who
know the situation can provide constructive insights and suggestions.

Thus, a faculty member, with input from students and colleagues, is in the best position to evaluate the quality of his or her
own teaching. A department is in the best position, perhaps with
the help of an outside consultant, to evaluate its curriculum.
There is, of course, a place for college-wide evaluation because
we are part of an institution that has an overall mission. These
college-wide evaluations will be best done when evaluations
have been effectively done at the individual and the department
levels. What is important is willingness to evaluate our work,
face the realities we find, and then respond with innovation and
creative work when change is needed to achieve the excellence to
which we aspire.

The same ideas and principles apply to all of our academic activities—advising, scholarship, research, and college and community service. At the college-wide level this has special
application to the curriculum and, in particular, to our overall requirements and the core curriculum. It is in this area that we most
visibly express our college-wide commitment to academic excellence. The Academic Affairs Board, provost, and the deans have
special responsibilities to ensure the quality and excellence of the
curriculum.

These important considerations regarding excellence and its
impact on momentum apply to every non-academic area of the
campus as well. The quality of our work in the Registrar's Office,
the Business Office, College Relations, Financial Aid, and Public
Safety, to name only some, has a direct impact on our attitudes
toward the College and enthusiasm for the future. Excellence is
an important key to maintaining momentum and this comes

through honest evaluation and creative, diligent efforts to improve.

In our concern for excellence, it is important to recognize the diversity of gifts in the College community, and that few persons can be excellent in everything they do. Thus, an important principle in achieving excellence is to enable persons to spend much of their time and energy in the areas where they have special strengths and abilities. For the faculty, the ideal environment for making such arrangements and assignments is the department. This means that planning and leadership at the department level is especially important. The objective should be to have each faculty member have goals and assignments that are challenging but reasonable, equitable, and which contribute to the goals of the department and the overall mission of the College. A covenant community provides a framework in which these matters can be openly and creatively addressed.

C. Refining the Organizational Structure

There are two dimensions in the organizational structure at Hope. One is the regular organizational structure of departments and divisions, through which most of the activities of the College are conducted and many decisions are made. It is important to recognize that through this organizational structure each member of the College community has the opportunity to be involved in important decisions, including many that influence the individual directly. Further, department chairs and department heads have the opportunity and responsibility to represent their departments on many matters as they are considered on a college-wide basis. Thus, at Hope the regular organizational structure is intended to have a strong emphasis on participation by all members of the College community.

At Hope we also have the Board and Committee system which was initiated in 1965 and has served remarkably well for twenty years. The strength of the system is the opportunity that faculty,

students, and administrators have to address matters together and
to make decisions that have college-wide significance. This is
particularly important in academic matters, since the faculty has
the primary responsibility for the curriculum, and the Academic
Affairs Board is an excellent vehicle to achieve this. Similarly,
the Campus Life Board provides an excellent forum to discuss issues relating to students and in making decisions about student
affairs. The effectiveness of the total organizational structure in
planning, operating, and administrating the various activities of
the College has an impact on the momentum of the College. If
these activities become burdensome, time consuming, or slow in
responding to issues, it can detract from the sense of forward momentum. We should not hesitate to evaluate all aspects of our organizational structure and fine-tune it where necessary, to assure
that it is functioning well and contributing to the ongoing momentum of the College.

Some have expressed concern about our governance system.
One concern is about the time required for participation. Another
is whether these assignments are shared equitably throughout the
community. A third concern is whether service on boards and
committees is adequately recognized in our merit system.

A few personal thoughts on this may help to stimulate our
thinking on these matters. Board and committee activities must
be carefully structured and delineated so that the work is effectively conducted. Perhaps the appropriate administrative officer
(for example, the dean of students for the Campus Life Board)
can handle much of the paperwork and can help to structure the
agenda and thereby assist the chair of a given board or committee.

We recognize that most faculty members must be involved in
advising and in some service activities at the department and/or
college levels. It is imperative that each faculty member's assignments be reasonable, so that there is adequate time for teaching
and scholarship. Further, though service on a board or committee

might replace other activities, it must never be a substitute for quality in teaching or scholarship.

It is important to recognize that the primary responsibility of new faculty members is to establish themselves as outstanding teachers and scholars. Thus, in most cases it is advisable for new faculty members to have light committee assignments, especially at the college level. This means, of course, that in making tenure decisions, the primary focus must be on teaching and scholarship. This also means that for older faculty members who carry major committee assignments, these must be considered an important contribution in our merit system.

One final observation. Our faculty and staff handbooks are important documents for setting forth specific information on a variety of matters. It is important that these be accurate, current, and as brief as possible. At the same time, we must recognize that in a covenant community our relationships, our mutual respect and support for each other, and our common goals provide the basis for creative problem solving, resolution of conflicts, and adapting to change. Our handbooks must be a servant and not a master.

D. Exercising Leadership

Leadership is also a key factor in maintaining momentum. One measure of effective leadership is the degree to which momentum is developed and maintained. In this regard also, momentum is a by-product of other qualities.

Leadership is exercised in many ways in the College setting. The professor is the leader in the learning environment that takes place in the classroom. Department chairpersons exercise leadership in many important ways. Further, there is a great deal of informal leadership that takes place throughout the College, in departments as well as in boards and committees. The Board of Trustees, and its officers and committee chairpersons, have special responsibilities for overall leadership in the College.

At this time the College is focusing special attention on the selection of a new president. The responsibilities of the president in the overall leadership of the College, and in the developing and maintaining of momentum are clearly recognized. This document has been written to assist in the selection of a new president, though it may have significance in other ways as well. At the Planning Retreat, we gave consideration to the qualities the College should seek in its new president at this time in its history. We recognized that the primary responsibility to establish these criteria rests with the Presidential Search Committee and the Board of Trustees. However, the thoughts expressed at the Planning Retreat are presented here as a contribution to this important effort.

1. One way of viewing the presidency of any organization is to see the responsibilities from three different perspectives—administration, management, and leadership. Administration involves keeping the organization functioning on an even keel, with efficiency, harmony, and sound policies and practices. Management involves securing and marshaling all the resources needed, human and physical, to accomplish the mission of the organization. Leadership involves establishing and articulating the mission of the organization, clarifying the value system under which the organization will operate, and developing the strategies and plans to fulfill the mission. All three of these dimensions are important qualities to seek in the president of any organization.

2. It is important to distinguish between leadership gifts and management skills. Leadership gifts are the most important qualities we should seek. While these can be nurtured and developed, they cannot be taught, for they relate to the character and basic qualities of the individual. In essence, leadership gifts relate to the question of "who I am." The personal values and basic commitments of the leader must coincide with the mission and values of the institution. In contrast, management experience in the new

president is very desirable, but to a significant extent these management skills can be taught. This distinction between management skills and leadership gifts must be kept in mind.

3. Some of the personal qualities we should seek in the new president are these:

a. the ability to inspire trust;

b. the willingness and ability to be a servant leader and to be compassionate;

c. a sound understanding and appreciation of the liberal arts, the mission of liberal arts colleges, and the unique blend of teaching with scholarship and research that we emphasize at Hope;

d. a mature understanding of and commitment to the Christian faith, both in its intellectual and experiential dimensions and in the implications of the Christian faith to higher education.

4. Some of the skills that will be desirable to have or the ability to develop are these:

a. the ability and willingness to be involved in fund-raising;

b. the ability to relate to all of our constituencies;

c. the ability to plan effectively for the future;

d. the ability to enhance the national reputation of the College. Because the physical plant will be in excellent condition, skills relating to campus development will be less important than those that relate to developing Hope's national reputation.

Other factors that relate to momentum can certainly be identified. Those cited above can serve to further our thinking on the importance of momentum to the future well-being of the College, and how the decisions we make today can influence the spirit of enthusiasm and sense of momentum that we pass on to our institutional heirs.

V.
CONCLUDING COMMENTS

A. *The Role of Outside Counsel and Advocates*

If we are to achieve our mission with the excellence to which we aspire, we not only need to give diligent, creative efforts to this task, but must also utilize the assistance of persons outside the College to give counsel and to serve as advocates. With the involvement of such persons, our own efforts can be more effectively directed and utilized. We must choose outside advocates who are experienced, well-qualified persons, and define their assignments so that they can make their contributions efficiently and effectively. Using capable outside advocates with a national reputation can also serve to enhance the national reputation of the College.

There are several different areas in which such outside counsel is appropriate.

1. Legal

More than a decade ago, the College retained the firm of Varnum, Riddering, Schmidt, and Howlett as our legal counsel. This fine Grand Rapids firm has given excellent service to the College and is an example of the value of retaining outstanding professional counsel when such services are needed.

2. Auditing

A thorough audit of the business and financial operation of the College by independent outside auditors is of vital importance, both for the internal operation of the College and to demonstrate to our constituents that the College is indeed well run. For more than a decade we have used the firm Deloitte, Haskins, and Sells. We have been well satisfied with their work, but the College may wish from time to time to review this commitment.

3. Site Planning and Architectural Work on Major Projects

This work should be done by nationally known architects who are capable of working effectively with the College.

4. Public Relations

Although our previous efforts at working with a national public relations firm were not as successful as we had hoped, our efforts to build a national reputation will be greatly furthered if we identify and retain a national public relations firm that can give us top-quality, professional help.

5. Financial Planning

Although we have considerable financial planning talent on the board, there may be occasions when an innovative financial advisor from the outside, who can operate at arms length, can be of significant help in developing broad financial strategies.

6. Real Estate Development

As we explore options regarding the development of the area surrounding the campus, we may find it helpful to retain someone who is well acquainted with various ways in which this area could be developed to the mutual benefit of both the city and the College. In some cases this might lead to cooperative arrangements with real estate developers who are interested in investing constructively on the margins of the campus.

7. Other Fields

We should give careful consideration to using a consultant from time to time in such areas as the academic program, admissions, residential life, community building, and strategic planning. A consultant of the caliber of Peter Drucker (who has made important contributions to many corporations) who would meet from time to time with the president and the senior administrative staff, could be of considerable help as we develop overall plans and strategies in our quest for excellence. Similarly, a person such as Bruce Heywood, who participated in the Senior Seminar Colloquium this past summer, could be of great help in evaluating our academic program and giving insights and suggestions on learning and the life of the mind.

B. Enhancing the National Reputation of the College

An important dimension of achieving our goals for excellence, enrollment, faculty, and financial resources is an enhanced national reputation for the College. To use a conventional term, this will involve building our national image. There are several basic factors we must keep in mind as we move forward in this endeavor.

1. Our effort for enhanced national image must be based on reality; it must not be contrived or achieved by manipulation. Our first responsibility is to develop the inherent qualities and strength of Hope College. Then a strong national reputation for Hope can be based on the genuine excellence that takes place at Hope. St. Paul's injunction, "Do not think of yourself more highly than you ought, but think of yourself with sober judgment," is certainly appropriate.

2. Our image is developed by everything we do—the scholarly publications and professional activities of the faculty; the experiences and accomplishments of our students; the quality of the buildings we build and the appearance of the campus; the voice and manner of our phone operators and receptionists; the promptness and quality of our communication; the impressions and information that visitors receive when they visit the campus. All these reflect the reality of what we are and do.

3. If we are to achieve the national reputation we seek, our efforts to have high quality in the ordinary activities cited above must be part of a deliberate plan and program to enhance the national reputation of the College. This plan will involve our publications, press releases, interactions with the media featuring

the president and members of the faculty and staff in media events, bringing distinguished visitors to the campus, and the involvement of the faculty and staff in professional organizations and other national bodies. We have already done well in this regard and we have many inherent strengths. However, to achieve our goals of a national reputation, we should utilize the services of an outstanding public relations consultant who can work with us in formulating a long-range plan to build the reputation of the College and in developing specific strategies to implement this.

4. We must be clear in our purpose for seeking an enhanced reputation. Pride is an ever-present danger, and the academic community is not without this tendency. Our efforts to enhance our national reputation must be perceived and undertaken in the light of our commitment to be servants—to serve students first of all and then the various communities and constituencies of which we are part. Our efforts to raise funds must be undertaken with a sense of stewardship and the responsibility to use these gifts to serve others. For us, this perspective is rooted in the Christian faith, which also gives the dynamic to achieve excellence and the grace to publicize the College wisely.

5. The cost for a program to develop a national reputation must be carefully weighed against the benefits. As in all other activities, we must be good stewards of our resources.

The overall plan by which we can proceed in this matter would be along these lines:

1. Give continued, diligent attention to achieving the highest quality we can in all we do.

2. Make a clear commitment to enhance the national reputation of the College.

3. Develop the in-house capabilities we need to build this national reputation.

4. Retain outside counsel that can help us formulate a plan to achieve our goal and strategies by which the plan can be implemented.

5. Make the campus community fully aware of the importance of enhancing our national reputation, why we are seeking to achieve this, and how we are proceeding.

C. Closing Comment

The preparation of this report has been a very rewarding experience, for it has enabled me to systematically think about many aspects of the College I have come to respect and love during the past thirteen years. My hope is that it will be a positive contribution in enabling Hope to become an ever stronger and more significant institution in the years ahead, even while it retains the perspective of serving students, the church, and the world, all to the glory of God.

Report to the Board of Trustees
October 1985

Retrospect

The final year of Van Wylen's presidency was a time of both re-
flection on the past and looking forward to a new era. In this last
"State of the College Address" the President shared his vision for
the College and offered a number of personal reflections.

It is a privilege to welcome each of you to the opening session of
this Pre-College Conference and to this new academic year. I extend a special welcome to those who have joined us in recent
months and are here for the first time. We are delighted that you
have cast your lot with us and are now a part of the Hope community as you work with us to fulfill the important mission we
have as a college. We hope your experiences with us and in this
community will be rewarding for you in every way.

I am mindful that this is the last State of the College address
that I will have the opportunity to present to you, and I suspect
that this is, to some extent, also on your minds today. However, I
do not want to make more of this than I should. The College will
certainly go on and I have confidence that it will go from strength
to strength. But having been intimately involved with the College
for the past fourteen years, and having grown to love Hope and
care deeply about it, I do have some thoughts I want to share with
you as we enter the last year that I will have the opportunity to
serve as your president.

THE FUTURE OF HOPE COLLEGE

Size of the College and Future Enrollment

For some time we have had as a goal to remain at our present
size. While this could be interpreted as a decision simply to retain
the status quo, there are several factors which make this a reasonable decision, as I have spelled out on several occasions. I

strongly urge again that we focus our energies on recruiting well-qualified students in such numbers that we retain our present size. We need, however, to recognize that in view of demographic factors, to achieve this goal over the next decade will be difficult. The number of high school graduates will continue to decrease until 1992, and even then will increase very slowly for several years. Thus, retaining our present enrollment will be a major undertaking and will require our best cooperative efforts.

One of our great strengths has been the active involvement of the entire College community, particularly the faculty, in our admissions program. It is vitally important that we continue this in the future, and I urge that we retain this dimension of our admissions program.

There are two other aspects of enrollment that I must briefly touch on. The first involves minority students. We are embarking on a new effort in this matter with the appointment of an assistant dean for Multicultural Life. I want to stress that our goal for an increased number of minority students must be a long-term effort, and not simply to do what is in vogue. Rather, our goal is, first of all, to serve these students to the best of our abilities. Further, we want to be a college that reflects in our student body and faculty the diversity of contemporary society. This is the world in which both we and our graduates must live and serve. We want to help our students prepare to live with a genuine sense of community in a diverse society, and see the power of Christian faith helping to achieve this goal.

As we increase the number of minority students, we may need to provide assistance for some of these students in their transition from high school to college. I do not propose that we initiate a specific program at this time, but we must be alert to this possible need and open to addressing it when it arises.

The second issue is financial aid, both need-based and merit-based. Financial aid has become both a need and an expectation of many students and an integral element of both admissions and retention. It has also become a very costly item. Last year our expenditures for financial aid were $2,200,000, which is ten percent of our Educational and General budget. The whole matter of need-based and merit-based financial aid will be one of the most important things to manage in the years ahead.

As I reflected on this, it seemed to me that there are three factors we should keep in mind.

1. Quality of the institution is always more important in admissions than financial aid. Only when we maintain high quality in all facets of our programs can financial aid help in admissions and retention.

2. It will be important to give continued attention to the balance between need-based and merit-based financial aid. Both are important and both must be supported, but the balance between the two must be such that we truly benefit our students. Further, the new emphasis on recruiting minority students may require additional need-based resources.

3. We must continue to explore creative ways to help families and students finance the student's education. Our new Alumni/Friends Tuition Program, which involves prepaid tuition, is one such effort. While loans will no doubt continue to be used by students, we must be careful that students are not saddled with too large a debt when they graduate. This whole matter of financing students' education is worthy of our thoughtful, creative efforts.

Finances

During my first years at Hope, two private institutions (the University of Richmond and Tulsa University) each received bequests of about $50 million. I have been eagerly opening the mail each day for the past fourteen years—and am still waiting.

If I were to put my perception of Hope's financial picture in a nutshell, it would be this. Hope's vision for excellence, and its achievement of this vision have, over the years, outstripped its financial resources. I want, first of all, to say that I think this is something of which we can be proud. It is rewarding to achieve more than is expected of us. It has also been rewarding to build the physical facilities and strive to acquire the financial resources needed to fulfill this vision. But to acquire the resources to close the gap between vision and reality is a very difficult task. Further, our vision and expectations tend to expand, as they probably should, so that even as resources are provided, the gap tends to remain.

This matter was brought to my attention in a rather striking way recently as I reviewed the publication *Voluntary Support of Education* for 1984-85. This report lists the gifts received by colleges during 1984-85 and the value of their endowment on June 30, 1985. What was especially interesting is that among Great Lakes Colleges Association colleges Hope had the largest income but has the smallest endowment.

While it would be great to receive a truly major gift, the only path we can responsibly follow is to work diligently to build our resources from traditional sources. As we do so, I have concluded that to achieve both present and long-term financial strength we must vigorously pursue three important activities in parallel. These involve the Annual Fund, the Endowment Fund, and programmatic support.

The Annual Fund will be the basis of providing additional resources in the short run. This past year we received $1,520,000 for the Annual Fund. With the completion of the Campaign, we will place a great deal of emphasis on the Annual Fund. This year the budget is $1,670,000. I believe that in a few years the Annual Fund can reach $2 million annually, and within five or six years $2,500,000 per year. If this goal can be achieved, this will provide significant resources to sustain and enhance the operation of the College and our commitment to excellence.

Secondly, we must continue to build the endowment. This will be done primarily through estate planning—annuities, trusts, and wills. A very significant program in planned giving has been built up over the last ten years and has been enhanced through the Campaign for Hope. This program provides opportunities for friends of the College to give significant resources to the College at a time when they are no longer needed. As of June 30, the market value of the endowment was $17,900,000. While this is small compared to many colleges, it has increased significantly and is now an important factor in our finances. Further, the prospect for steady growth in the endowment fund is very good.

The third is to vigorously seek funds for various programmatic activities. This includes federally supported programs such as the National Science Foundation (NSF), the National Endowment for Humanities (NEH), and the National Institute of Health, state funds such as the Michigan Council for the Arts and the Michigan Council for the Humanities, and a variety of foundations.

If we vigorously pursue these three approaches to fund-raising, I believe that the financial strength of the College can steadily increase in the years ahead. It will be particularly helpful that the need for physical facilities should decrease significantly after the library and certain related projects are completed. However, the need to carefully allocate resources will be with us for the indefinite future.

We need to remind ourselves that we have a great reservoir of goodwill and positive support for the College. We also have a good reputation among various funding agencies such as NSF and NEH and a number of foundations. The challenge before us is to continually build and strengthen these relationships, provide ways in which people can have a genuine sense of ownership of the College, and provide effective vehicles for persons and organizations to support the College.

Facilities

As I reflect on my years at Hope, I realize that a good deal of my energies have been devoted to campus development. It is interesting, against this background, to note that in the discussions I had prior to my coming to Hope, the matter of campus development was not discussed extensively. At that time the De Witt Center had just been completed and construction of the Peale Science Center was under way. The need for a new physical education center was, as I recall, the only specific matter discussed. The need for this facility, as those who remember the Carnegie-Schouten Gymnasium will attest, was well understood and accepted. No other facilities beyond the new physical education center were projected. I recall telling persons and foundations, as we were raising funds for this center, that this was the last major building Hope needed.

As we know, this was not the case. The results of our campus development program are well known to us, and we need not dwell at length on them. What I do want to focus on is some general principles that I learned over these years and that I believe will be important in the future.

The first is the importance of having an attractive campus. I recall a conversation before I came to Hope with a nationally known educator who knows Hope well and visits the campus frequently. He had been on Hope's campus recently and told me that to him the campus looked rather shabby. I believe that we articulate our values and our commitment to quality in non-verbal ways through the appearance of the campus and, on hearing this comment, I determined to do what I could to make this campus an expression of our commitment to excellence. I also recall taking walks with Margaret down 12th Street and visualizing the potential for greatly enhancing the beauty of the campus if this street could be closed.

Today we have a campus that almost every visitor acclaims as being exceptionally attractive and well maintained. It is truly a splendid place to work, and what a joy it is to show the campus to visitors, alumni, and prospective students! I believe this attractiveness has contributed significantly to our successes in admissions and fund-raising.

The second lesson is that whenever we undertake a project, we should do it well. If we do, it will better fulfill the function for which it was constructed, and in most cases will be more economical in the long run.

Many of us recall the occasion during my first or second year at Hope when a ceiling in a classroom in Van Raalte came down. Fortunately, there was enough warning so the class could vacate this room. A few years later, the ceiling in Snow Auditorium came down. We were grateful that this took place at a time when the room was vacant. These were vivid reminders of the importance of quality.

When the Dow Center was designed, we had to decide whether to put cement blocks or brick on the interior walls. We decided to spend the extra money for brick interiors, both to enhance its beauty and to reduce long-term maintenance. I believe that as we look at this building after eight years of intensive use, we would all agree that this was a good decision.

It is my conclusion that if design is tied closely to function, with an emphasis on quality, we will achieve the most for our construction dollars and have long-term satisfaction and economies.

The third lesson is that when undertaking a project to build a new facility, we should be certain that need and function are carefully articulated, evaluated, and communicated to the architect. This clearly implies having those who will use the facility actively involved in the design. I believe we have done a good job of this over the years, particularly through the development of Program Statements. Having the users involved doesn't mean that each person will get exactly what was requested, but it does mean that each request is carefully evaluated in the light of the · overall requests and constraints. One word of caution. We must carefully evaluate requests to spend large sums for specialized research facilities. Because the interests of the faculty member involved might change, a careful evaluation of the cost-benefits of the space and its potential for alternate uses should be considered in the design process.

Academic

As I wrote this section of the report, I realized that this is an area in which I have relatively few comments and suggestions. The reason is quite simple. Academically, the College is exceptionally strong. Further, I sense a creative, dynamic spirit that bodes well for continued academic vitality. I also reminded myself, as I reflected on the strength of this aspect, that this was the area in which I have had the least direct involvement over the years.

It seems to me that the essential key to achieving and maintaining academic strength lies in recruiting well-qualified and well-motivated persons for the faculty, supporting and encouraging faculty members as individuals and in their work, and in creating an environment in which the faculty can work creatively and effectively together. The success we have achieved, which is very substantial indeed, is due in significant measure to the extent to which we have reached these goals.

I again want to commend you as individuals and as a faculty for your accomplishments as teachers/scholars, for your great interest in and commitment to your students, and for all you are as persons. Having you as colleagues and friends, observing and applauding your accomplishments, and seeing the impact you have on your students, have been some of the most rewarding experiences I have had at Hope. Thank you for all you have achieved and for all you have done to enhance the academic strength and reputation of the College.

There are a few academic matters I wish to comment on briefly.

1. International Education

There are two aspects of international education—having Hope students study abroad and having foreign students study at Hope.

Both are of vital importance. Under the leadership of Paul Fried and Neal Sobania, our international program has flourished and become an integral part of college life. However, the importance of our international educational programs, and of enhancing an international perspective throughout the College, will increase in the years ahead. The reason, of course, is simply that the nature of the world in which we live requires this perspective. The challenge will be to develop programs so that these opportunities are available to students at reasonable cost, do not require undue expenditure of College resources, and are effective learning experiences.

International students who study at Hope are an important resource for enhancing the international perspective and multicultural life of the College. This fall we will have discussions on how we can more effectively recruit international students.

Because an overseas experience is very enriching for students from this country, we must encourage and enhance these opportunities for our students without detracting from the strength of our on-campus programs. This will need continued creative attention.

2. Continuing Education

For a considerable period of time we have been discussing what role we should play in continuing education in this community. There are continuing education needs in this area. We are meeting some of them, other institutions are meeting certain needs, and some needs are unmet. Davenport has a fairly extensive program in our community, and Aquinas College has explored the possibility of our offering its master in management program in Holland. There is also a fine consortium of public school programs in community education.

What we should do, in my judgment, is stake out the role we are willing to play, move ahead and do this well, and encourage other institutions to meet other needs. Further, I believe that the new library offers some interesting possibilities to develop programs in "continued learning," in which the emphasis is on individual responsibility to continue to learn, as compared to "continuing education," in which the focus is on institutions giving and students taking courses. Also, the need for primary and secondary teachers to take courses in order to retain their certification offers some interesting opportunities for us to meet needs in this area.

3. Honors Programs

Another area we have been discussing for some time is an honors program. Almost without exception, there is agreement that we should have such a program.

In my judgment, an honors program could have two components. The first would be a program for the very best students. Such a program would serve the top one or two percent of the students in any given class and would be designed to prepare students to compete for Marshall, Rhodes, and comparable scholarships. This program would start in the freshman year and continue throughout the students' undergraduate years. While students could apply for this program, selection standards would be such that the purpose and integrity of the program is maintained. This program could well involve a group of faculty members in a somewhat informal organization with an appropriate name and identity.

The second would be a general honors program that would be more traditional and would provide challenges and opportunities for approximately the top ten percent of the class. This program would primarily involve special curricular opportunities and related academic advising.

I believe that having such a program would provide unique opportunities for our most gifted students and enable us to attract an increased number of outstanding high school students. This program could also have a positive influence on retention. As we move into these areas, we will have to give attention to how this would relate to our current programs for Presidential and National Merit scholars, our Distinguished Scholars program, and on students who are not in an honors program. We must avoid developing a spirit of elitism or any suggestion that students who are not in the honors program are second class.

4. Freshman Studies and Institutional Research

For some time I have had a concern about freshman studies, namely, how we can best take into account the diversity in preparation that students have as they come to Hope. On the one hand we have the FOCUS program and, as I have just suggested, there is the possibility of an honors program. These programs will certainly help us address this issue. But there is a more general problem which relates to the diversity in academic qualities and personal preparation for college studies that students have as they come to us. These diversities relate to the quality of the high school which the student attended, the performance in the given high school, the student's native ability, and the student's motivation. There are students attending Hope who clearly have the ability to succeed well at Hope and have done well in high school, but whose preparation is not strong because of the quality of the high school attended. The primary need of such students is an effective transition period during their first, and perhaps second, semester. On the other hand, there are students who have strong native ability, who attended a good high school, and who only did an adequate job because they lacked motivation. These students offer a special challenge to us to provide an environment in which they will begin to realize their full potential. These are but two examples of the variety of qualifications and attitudes students have as they come to Hope.

There is much we could do by way of institutional research to analyze these differences. We could identify the qualities students have as they come to college, analyze their performance in relation to these qualifications, and then seek to develop freshman-year programs that are in significant measure responsive to where students are as they come to Hope. There would be no difference in graduation requirements. We would only seek to be responsive to where students are as they come to us and provide an appropriate transition for their college work. This might even have implications as to where we assign students in the residence halls. To achieve this overall goal, we would need some effective academic research so that we can gain insights and understandings as to what the major variables are that we should look for, and how we can provide the best freshman year for students to begin to achieve their full potential. This whole area could become an interesting research area for a faculty member who had an interest in the theory and practice of learning.

Residential and Extra-Curricular Activities

There are many facets of college life that are involved in this general category, including all of the activities of the Office of Student Affairs.

In this area also I sense that overall things are going well. An important issue is, as I see it, the quality of residential life. This is also one of the most difficult areas to effectively administer and manage. While many aspects of our residential life are going well, there are certainly significant opportunities for improvement. The student affairs staff is addressing a number of these and I know this will be a priority endeavor for them this year.

The goal is quite clear—to create an environment in the residence halls in which students have a genuine sense of ownership of their life and the quality of life. Then under the leadership of the staff, they can work cooperatively to make our residence halls places where high academic achievement is encouraged and promoted, where value-oriented personal development is enhanced, and where interpersonal skills and friendships are developed. I believe we can look forward to a new level of quality in residential life this year and, through this, to improved quality in academic achievement.

There is one additional matter in regard to campus life. When I came to Hope in 1972, which was just after the peak of the student activism of the late 1960s and early 1970s, the Higher Horizon program was flourishing, and the Ministry of Christ's People had a number of activities that provided opportunities for students, faculty, and staff to reach out and serve others. Our Upward Bound program, which has been very successful over the years, was initiated in this same era. While many of these volunteer activities continue, they have, I believe, lost some of their vitality and appeal to students. I believe that a renewal of the spirit of voluntary service, a vision for meeting the needs of people, and a rejuvenation of these programs, would be a very significant step for us as a College to take at this time. As the student affairs staff moves in this direction, I hope it will have broad support from the faculty and the entire College community.

THE CHANGE IN THE PRESIDENCY

This morning I want to share a few thoughts about the change in the presidency at Hope. I have no direct responsibilities in the screening, evaluation, and selection process. My purpose in sharing these thoughts is simply to do what I can to promote an environment in which this will be the best possible process.

The first thought is that this is, quite naturally, a time of uncertainty for all. Who will it be? What impact will this change have on me? What kind of leader will this person be? How will the College change under this person's leadership? These are reasonable questions, but there is no way of answering them before the events begin to take shape. There is no ultrasound to give us a picture of the yet-to-be-named president. So, uncertainty and some anxiety are quite natural.

Can anything helpful be said about this uncertainty? To urge that we have confidence and faith, and that we remember this matter in our prayers, while certainly very true, is not fully responsive to these feelings. The best thing we can do for the new president and for the College is to have the strongest possible operations in place throughout the College, with well-qualified and well-motivated people in each position, and to retain a clear sense of mission. The stronger the College is when the new president arrives, the easier it will be for this person to assume leadership, and begin to work with all the constituencies of the College. And, of course, this will also be the very best for us as a College.

What about the interview process when the candidates come to the campus? I don't know what the process will be, but I do know that this is a difficult process—for the interviewers and the interviewee. Those doing the interviewing obviously want to get the most complete understanding of the individual they can, and this involves asking and answering questions in a frank and open manner. For the one being interviewed, it is difficult to answer the wide range of questions that can be asked. Some questions require a more comprehensive answer than time allows, and when one does not know the person asking the question, it is impossible to know the nuances behind the questions. All of these things make the interview process difficult. It is also important to remember that the person being interviewed is eager to gain an impression of the College, about the people who are here, and Hope's potential for the future. Thus, in the interview process, we are also selling the College.

I urge that whatever form the interview takes, it be done as graciously and as openly as possible. I still recall how confused and low I felt as Margaret and I drove back to Ann Arbor the evening of the day I was interviewed at Hope. In many ways it had been an unnatural dialogue. I had answered many questions poorly, especially the hypothetical ones, which are always difficult to answer. I wasn't at all sure that I was right for Hope and that Hope was right for me. In that context I remember with special appreciation the kind and gracious words that a few persons spoke to me that day, and how much these meant to me. I also know it is difficult to size up a person in an interview, since it is not the natural situation in which people work and relate to each other. This is why it is so important to find out all one possibly can about how a person has performed and related to people in prior positions. This gives the best indication of how that person would perform here.

I also want to say a few words about the situation when this new person begins to serve as president. This is a very difficult time for a new president, especially if this person comes from the outside. At that point, you don't know people, you don't know the ways and attitudes in which things are done, and you don't know what are the important things to do. In a very short period of time you meet many people from within and without the College, and you try to keep all the responsibilities and relationships straight. At the same time, people are watching you and weighing your words. I recall that one of my first impressions at Hope was that people weighed each word very carefully, and a casual comment was interpreted as having a deep, philosophical meaning. For me, my first years at Hope were the most difficult I have had in my life. I recall coming home from an evening faculty meeting during the second semester of my first year at Hope and saying to Margaret that I didn't think I could do the job.

The point of all of this is not simply to try to make it easy for the new president during the first few years, though some effort in this regard is certainly appropriate. Rather, it is simply to urge that we recognize that this is a difficult period. I hope that you will do all you can to have an understanding of the situation the new president is in, give encouragement whenever possible, gracious counsel when this seems advisable and, to the greatest extent possible, reserve judgment until the initial period is over.

The final point I want to make is that this person will be different, perhaps very significantly, from me. She or he will do things and react to things much differently than I do. This is good, and is as it should be, and will be a great asset to the College. It will be important for all of us to let the new president be his or her own person. We have been together for fourteen years now and have become accustomed to each other. While I sometimes wish I could do things in fresh and different ways, I know that I'm fairly predictable—regrettably so sometimes! It will be exciting and challenging to have a new voice, new mannerisms, and fresh ideas and momentum. This will be good for the College.

SOME PERSONAL OBSERVATIONS

Many of you have asked me about how I feel as I begin this last academic year and what things stand out in my mind as I look back, and what our plans are for the future. As I comment on a few of these matters, I want to stress that this is not my swan song. That will come when this year is over and not as we begin it.

The first thing I want to say is that I have thoroughly enjoyed my years at Hope and I am deeply grateful for the privilege of serving as your president. At the same time, I am convinced that both for the College and myself, this is the right time for me to retire. I look forward to serving this year, and I look forward to leaving these responsibilities to another person when the year is over. So I have complete peace about this year and my approaching retirement.

What things stand out in my mind as I look back? I will share a few thoughts with you, partly to give some background to those who have joined us in the last decade, and partly to share a bit of myself with all of you.

The Great Impact That a Few Key Decisions
Have on Our Lives

I recall the great struggle Margaret and I had as to whether or not we should accept the invitation to come to Hope. The Search Committee decided to recommend my appointment to the board, but before doing so wanted assurance that I would accept if invited. Margaret and I struggled with that decision for a month and then had to ask for an extension when we couldn't decide. We were happy in Ann Arbor, and had recently built a home we planned to live in for most of the rest of our lives. Our entire family enjoyed the schools, the community, our church life, and other activities in Ann Arbor, and the overall situation was fully satisfactory to us. We had children in the eleventh, ninth, and eighth grades, as well as one in college, and a third grader, so it was a rather difficult time to move. On the other hand, we came to recognize Hope as an outstanding academic institution, with a solid record of accomplishment and great potential for the future. We could see that coming here would be a very stimulating, significant challenge.

When we finally made the decision to come, it was much more in response to what we sensed as a call, and because we believed this was the right thing to do, rather than arriving at anything that approached a rational decision. What made this such a difficult decision was that, as far as I can recall, at no other time in my life had I made a major decision on such a subjective basis.

Looking back now, I am deeply grateful that we made the decision to come to Hope, or perhaps I should say that we were led to this decision. This has been a tremendous learning, growing, and rewarding experience for me. How much I would have missed if I had played it safe and stayed in Ann Arbor. I think of all the friendships I have made with persons here in this room, as well as in the community and throughout the country with alumni. So I am deeply grateful to God for the privilege of having been at Hope for these past fourteen years and to each of you for all you have meant to me. In retrospect, I am not sure why it was such a difficult decision to make in the first place.

How Little I Knew What Is Involved in Serving as President

On occasion I am asked by a student what a president does. I am always embarrassed by the way I fumble in answering that question. It sounds as if I am struggling to make something up to justify my being here. This does remind me, however, of how little I understood about the job of being president when I came to Hope. I certainly didn't grasp the wide range of constituencies and organizations one has to relate to—the Board of Trustees, alumni, the RCA denomination and individual congregations, the community, organizations such as the GLCA, MCF, AICUM, MIAA, in addition to all the faculty and student interactions and organizations. I didn't realize the vital role the president plays in fund-raising and how much involvement of the president is required in a successful fund-raising program. I didn't realize the great volume of mail that crosses one's desk and how many letters are required to answer this mail. I didn't realize how much time and energy is required to translate dreams and ideas into realities. All of this has made these years a tremendous learning experience, provided opportunities for a lot of hard, creative work, and offered many opportunities to have a sense of accomplishment.

The Value of Stability

As I look back at my years at Hope, it seems to me they were divided into a period of four years of getting started, and ten years of relative stability. As many of you know, I came to Hope in 1972 after the College had been without a president for two years. During those two years the board had launched a major capital campaign (the Build Hope Campaign), and I was handed the assignment to complete this—successfully! During the six-month period between the time I was appointed president and arrived on campus, the vice president for Business and Finance resigned, which was to be effective the day I arrived on campus. During this same period the campus representative of the outside fund-raising consultant for the Build Hope Campaign and the vice president for Development had major conflicts, with the result that three weeks after I arrived, the vice president for Development resigned. After my first year at Hope, the dean for Academic Affairs resigned effective at the end of the second year. I struggled with the question of what would be the most effective organization for the College. All of these made my first years at Hope a very difficult time.

I am very grateful that during my first week at Hope, Bill Anderson agreed to serve as vice president for Business and Finance and Barry Werkman as business manager. We have now been together for fourteen years and these two men have given superb leadership to the business operation of the College. During my second year, David Marker was appointed provost and he served very effectively for nine years and now Jack Nyenhuis is carrying on this work in a wonderful manner. The position I found most difficult to fill was that of vice president for Development. After my third year at Hope, I asked Bob De Young, who was serving as vice president for Student Affairs, to take on this responsibility. He accepted and now has done a marvelous job for the last eleven years. When Bob assumed this position, Mike Gerrie was appointed dean of students and served well in this capacity for eight years. During this period the place of admissions became increasingly important, and we decided that the dean for admissions should report directly to the president. I'm grateful that since 1978 Phil Fredrickson and James Bekkering have given effective leadership to the Admissions Office. Also, the organizational structure of divisional deans, though many had questions about it when it was instituted, has, I believe, served us very well.

Thus, it really took four years to fill the key administrative positions and develop a spirit of unity as a team. I am very grateful that for the past ten years we have had a great deal of stability, for this has enabled us to move forward in many different

areas to strengthen the College. We have accomplished a great
deal and we have much to be grateful for. To all those with
whom I have had the privilege of working directly, I extend a
special word of appreciation. I also extend my deep gratitude to
each of you, for you have given so generously of yourselves to
develop a wonderful learning, caring community, and a vision of
what we wanted to achieve. You have worked willingly, cooperatively, and diligently to accomplish so much.

Are there some things that stand out as accomplishments of
special significance? One must be very careful in citing accomplishments, for the line between gratitude and pride is fine
indeed. But there are a few items that I reflect on with special
gratitude. Each of these is the result of the commitment and work
of the entire College community and our constituencies and, thus,
the gratitude—and the pride—belong to all of us.

1. Campus Development

As I mentioned, when we were mutually exploring the possibility
of my coming to Hope, the matter of campus development was
not discussed in any serious way. So when I came to Hope I did
not visualize being involved in an extensive building program.

In many ways the building projects of the past fourteen years
have simply evolved. When the Peale Science Center was
completed, it was only natural to renovate the old science building, which we did, and named it Lubbers Hall. Then we were
able to proceed with the Dow Center. I remember so well the
phone call I received from Ted Doan of The Herbert H. and
Grace A. Dow Foundation, telling us that we had been awarded a
grant for this project. What made this call especially memorable
was that we had originally submitted a proposal for $500,000
which was declined. A year later we submitted a proposal again,
but this time for $300,000. When I received the call, I understood
Ted to say we had received a grant for $500,000. But as I stam-
mered my gratitude, I wasn't sure whether I had heard correctly

and I was too embarrassed to ask him to repeat it. But it was for $500,000, and later the foundation added another $500,000 for endowment to operate this facility. This fine facility was built just before the period of high inflation at the remarkably low cost of $3,700,000.

We then tackled the renovation of Van Vleck Hall and the expansion of the dining hall, both of which were much-needed projects. It is great to have Van Vleck Hall, the original College building, functioning today as a very useful and attractive building.

By this time I was beginning to enjoy doing such projects— the engineering genes were not totally dormant—and there were some real needs. One of these was Voorhees Hall. When we moved into the President's Home in 1972, we looked out at a Voorhees Hall which had been condemned by the fire marshall as unsafe as a student residence hall and had therefore been relegated to use as faculty offices. Though it was basically a fine building, it was rapidly becoming more and more run down. We tried to identify the best use for this facility, and finally concluded that we should renovate it and use it for its original purpose. Since that time it has become a very fine residence hall for upperclass students.

The loss of Van Raalte by fire in April 1980 did solve the question of what to do with that building! I recall that I frequently looked at Van Raalte Hall, wondering what to do with it. In many ways it was the front door to the College, and rather a shabby one indeed. But the fire removed that question and created the need to provide new administrative facilities, which we proceeded to do through the renovation of the De Witt Center. It grieved me to spend so much money reworking a building which was only twelve years old, but I believe that we all agree that it is a much more functional facility than it was originally.

When the Sligh Furniture Factory became available, we were able to develop a very fine art facility and to provide space for the physical plant department. And along the way there were various other projects—the underground power distribution system which eliminated unsightly poles on campus and enabled us to purchase electricity at a lower rate, installation of our own telephone system, installing an elevator in Dimnent Chapel, renovation of Durfee Hall and the Fraternity Complex, upgrading our computer resources, and construction of the College East residence hall. And, of course, the Maas Center and the new library are now under construction, projects which we were not even talking about ten years ago.

But this program of construction simply evolved in response to need and opportunities. Today our campus is exceptionally fine, and this is due to the effective work of many, many persons—architects, builders, tradesmen, donors, as well as faculty, staff, and students. These are accomplishments in which we can all take pride.

2. Faculty Scholarship

Another area in which I have a special sense of gratitude is the accomplishments of the faculty in scholarship. Hope had a strong tradition of scholarship and research in the sciences for many years. The Sloan Foundation grant in the late 1960s gave the entire science program a tremendous boost. But scholarly work in other areas had not developed as far. One of the most significant grants Hope has received during my years at Hope was a $160,000 from the Andrew W. Mellon Foundation in 1974. This was a four-year grant to support faculty development. Through these funds we initiated the Summer Faculty Grant Program, which has operated since that time. This emphasis on scholarship has permeated every facet of our academic program and is one of the reasons that today Hope is such an exciting place to be. Nothing succeeds like success, of course, and we have now received a significant number of grants from a variety of foundations and government agencies. A $150,000 challenge grant from the Andrew W. Mellon and the William and Flora Hewlett foundations six years ago was matched by $450,000 in other contributions to provide a $600,000 endowment fund, which is known as the President's Discretionary Fund for Self-Renewal. Much of the income from this fund is used to maintain this faculty development program.

This emphasis on scholarship has come to rich fruition in recent years, with the publication of some twenty-five books and many journal articles by members of the faculty. As another example, I cite the fact that this year four of our six faculty members in the physics department have received NSF research grants. Many other evidences of this outstanding record of faculty scholarship could be cited. This is an area of accomplishment in which I can properly have pride, since it is your accomplishments and not mine.

3. Clarifying Our Mission and Developing a Sense of Community

The third area that I can reflect on with a special sense of gratitude is that as we have worked together, we have clarified, in a real sense, the mission of the College, and that we have developed a genuine sense of community around this mission. I am well aware that there continue to be discussions about the mission of the College and that there are some who disagree with the Christian perspective of this mission or the way in which it is implemented. But I believe that overall a very significant, common vision of what we want to be as a college has emerged. This vision has the balance, about which we have spoken often, of both informed Christian commitment and a spirit of freedom and openness of inquiry. We also have a healthy diversity in our church affiliations, theological perspectives, and patterns of life, while acknowledging a common faith through Jesus Christ. I am deeply grateful for this rich sense of common purpose. Closely related to this is the sense of fellowship and community we

enjoy. This is evident in many ways, but in the past few months I
have been particularly struck by the wonderful relationships we
have with one another as we support our colleagues and their
families in a time of sorrow. As I have seen you in these circumstances, I have been deeply impressed with the genuine love and
care and support we give to one another in our community, and
in very substantial ways our students become a part of the same
caring, loving, and worshiping community.

Recently I have been struck with the tremendous diversity in
the ways in which people assert that they are working out the
Christian faith in practice. Recently I saw photographs of neo-
Nazis in uniform carrying their Bibles. The activities of the
political/religious right are well known to us. On the other hand,
we have contemporary liberation theology and revolution in the
name of Christianity. One of our graduates, who is doing doctoral
work in a major seminary, told me that no one could be appointed to their faculty without the support of the Gay Union at
this seminary. I mention these things not to judge any person, but
to say that it is in the midst of this wide diversity that I see a great
challenge for us as Christians at Hope College to demonstrate the
profound implications of the Christian faith, when it is thoughtfully understood and applied, for developing a sense of self-
worth, and for determining our values and our purpose in life.
There is also the challenge before us corporately to influence our
culture, and to be salt and light in contemporary society, and to
do this with humility and grace. It is in this context that the College's mission continues to fill me with enthusiasm and gratitude.

These are some of the things for which I am grateful.

There are also matters for which I have genuine regrets, for I
know I have made mistakes. I have at times offended people and
have not always carried out my responsibility in developing positive relationships. There have been times when I should have
spoken and didn't, and times when I did speak and should have
remained silent. These matters I regret, and for any apologies not

made earlier, I express them at this time. I trust that together we
will know the joy and peace that mutual forgiveness in Christ
brings to us.

One final comment. In my devotions recently, I read from the
Old Testament the verse that was a theme in the movie *Chariots
of Fire*. "The person who honors me I will honor." Together we
have as a college tried to honor God. We have not, as we know,
done this perfectly, and we have failed. But permeating our life
together has been a commitment to be faithful to God and to his
grace to us in Jesus Christ. And we know we have been richly
blessed. I have recounted some of these blessings, and together
we could multiply these a thousandfold.

This morning I want to thank you for your partnership in our
common faith, and acknowledge my own gratitude to God for his
goodness and grace to me personally and to us as a college. My
aspiration for you and for Hope College is that we will, in ever
fresh and vital ways, honor God and, in turn, receive through his
grace continued strength and wisdom and resources for the future.

Most years I have opened this address with a reading from
Scripture. This year I will close with a reading from the first and
fourth chapters from St. Paul's letter to the church at Philippi.

> I thank my God every time I remember you. In all my
> prayers for all of you, I always pray with joy because of your
> partnership in the gospel from the first day until now, being
> confident of this, that he who began a good work in you will
> carry it on to completion until the day of Christ Jesus.

> It is right for me to feel this way about all of you, since I
> have you in my heart; for whether I am in chains or defending
> and confirming the gospel, all of you share in God's grace with
> me. God can testify how I long for all of you with the affection
> of Christ Jesus.

> And this is my prayer: that your love may abound more and
> more in knowledge and depth of insight, so that you may be

able to discern what is best and may be pure and blameless until the day of Christ, filled with the fruit of righteousness that comes through Jesus Christ—to the glory and praise of God.

*   *   *   *   *

Rejoice in the Lord always. I will say it again: Rejoice! Let your gentleness be evident to all. The Lord is near. Do not be anxious about anything, but in everything, by prayer and petition, with thanksgiving, present your requests to God. And the peace of God, which transcends all understanding, will guard your hearts and your minds in Christ Jesus.

Finally, brothers, whatever is true, whatever is noble, whatever is right, whatever is pure, whatever is lovely, whatever is admirable—if anything is excellent or praiseworthy—think about such things. And the God of peace will be with you.

I said this would not be a swan song, but on reading this over and reflecting on it, it certainly sounds like a long overture to a swan song. But the overtures for many operas are much better known than the operas themselves. This being so, I have concluded that in view of this long overture, no swan song will be necessary.

Thank you for your patience in listening to me.

State of the College Address
August 1986

Basic Christian Faith

A student article on the "exclusivity" of the Christian faith became an occasion to make a theological point about creation and redemption and to explore the implications of this theology for a Christian liberal arts college.

The thoughtful article by Larry Wagenaar in his column LEFT OF CENTER in the November 5 issue of *The Anchor* prompted me to reflect on the important issues he raised. In this article I will share these with *Anchor* readers.

This reflection deals primarily with Mr. Wagenaar's basic premise which he states as follows: "The basic tenet of the faith is its exclusivity; one must be a Christian to be saved."

This is not my perception of the basic principle of the faith. (I am not sure it is wise to talk about "the" basic tenet. The faith is, in my judgment, all-embracing and difficult to reduce to a single principle. However, in this response I will follow the approach of Mr. Wagenaar.)

In my judgment, the basic tenet is twofold: this is God's world and he cares deeply about us and every part of his creation, and, secondly, God is redeeming the world through Christ. God created this world (over periods of time and in ways we do not fully understand); he created us in his image so that we can live in fellowship with him, have caring, supporting relationships with one another, and exercise special responsibilities to care for his creation.

The fundamental issue we face is, how can we accomplish this? The Christian gospel is that as a person comes to know and trust Jesus Christ, one can truly know God, and out of this relationship with him begin thoughtfully and seriously to look at life from God's point of view. This has inward dimension as we seek to become the person God intends us to be. But it has wonderful outward dimension, as we look at life from God's point of view, with his purposes and values in mind. All of life opens up to us as worthy of our careful study and development. Science becomes an opportunity to study the marvels and wonders of the physical and biological creation; psychology and sociology to understand something of ourselves and how we relate to each other; literature, art, and music to enjoy the remarkable accomplishments of persons God created. The basic tenet is not exclusivity. Rather, it is our responding to God in his marvelous acts of creation and his self-giving love to us in Jesus Christ. Rightly understood, the Christian faith can provide a marvelous framework for the very best in liberal arts education.

I believe we tend to err in two ways. The first is to think of Christianity almost exclusively in individual terms, of "my" being saved, of "my" being prepared to enter heaven. These are valid and biblical ideas, and should not be quickly set aside. A person who is on a path of self-destruction because of greed, drugs, or simply because of not knowing who he or she is, and is turned around through an encounter with Christ, may well speak of this experience as being "saved." But soon thereafter the focus should not be on being saved, but on living in a relationship with God with the joy, celebration, and purpose this brings. In a healthy marriage, the focus is not on the courtship and wedding of earlier years, but on a joyful, purposeful life that is lived in vital, dynamic relationship with each other. So it should be in our relationship to God and our walk as Christians.

The second error we may have is to not think broadly and creatively enough about the implications of the Christian faith for the liberal arts. The key, I believe, is to give proper perspective to the themes of both creation and redemption. If this is God's world, every part of it is worthy of our best efforts to understand it, and if God is working to redeem his people in this world from the impact of greed and selfishness, we ought to be co-workers with him in accomplishing this. And if God has endowed us with creative gifts, we should be using them to enrich life through such activities as music, art, and literature.

I see such things happening in significant measure at Hope. I think of Professor Smoot in her study of fossils, and Professor Greij beginning a magazine for bird watchers; I see Professor Dickie and her students studying how the tragedy of child abuse can be responsibly addressed, and Professor Verhey's study of the ethical issues we are confronted with as a result of modern medicine; I see the creative works of our music, art, dance, and theater faculty and students. Further, not only are the works of God worthy of our best study, but also the works of humans, the crown of God's creation, and that is why literature, philosophy, and history have such a vital place at a liberal arts college such as Hope. I believe we need to expand our understanding and vision of how the Christian faith can inspire and encourage us to the very best in liberal arts education. Then the Christian faith can be our ally and a marvelous resource in our pursuit of excellence in liberal arts education.

Recently, The Carnegie Foundation for the Advancement of Teaching released the results of a major national study and evaluation of undergraduate education. The report is entitled, "College: The Undergraduate Experience in America." The general conclusion of this report is: "The undergraduate college, the very heart of higher learning, is a troubled institution." One particular reason is cited:

> Many undergraduate colleges have lost their sense of mission. They are confused about how to impart shared values on which the vitality of both higher education and society depend. The disciplines have fragmented themselves into smaller and smaller pieces, and undergraduates find it difficult to see patterns in their courses and to relate what they learn to life. Archibald MacLeish observed in 1920, "There can be no educational postulates as long as there are no generally accepted postulates of life itself," and colleges appear to be

searching for meaning in a world where diversity, not commonality, is the guiding vision.

In the section on recommendations of this matter, the following statement is made:

> If the college experience is to be worthwhile, there must be intellectual and social values that its members hold in common, even as there must be room for private preference; a balance must be struck between two powerful traditions—individualism and community.

As I read this report and its recommendations, I was convinced anew that we have a marvelous context for our pursuit of excellence in liberal arts education.

A final comment. I do not deny that there is a measure of "exclusivity" in the Christian faith. But this is true in all of life. This is simply the consequence of many of our decisions. Marriage brings a strong sense of exclusivity. The two belong to each other in a way they can never relate to another person. Acknowledging Jesus Christ as our Lord and Savior has definite consequences, and brings us into a special relationship with those who share this faith. But if I understand the Bible correctly, the emphasis is not on the exclusivity, but on helping us to see the consequences of our choices, and encouraging us to receive with gratitude God's gifts in nature and grace.

Hope College, *The Anchor*
December 10, 1986

Letters

The files of a college president's office are crammed with correspondence: letters to government officials dealing with state education policies, and to heads of foundations, explaining the worthiness of Hope College to receive a grant; thousands of thank you notes to contributors; even notes to concerned parents about a course or a roommate. Here we present just a few letters to indicate the variety and scope of the correspondence. In some cases we have included the names of the correspondents, in others it seemed best to delete the names, to preserve confidentiality.

Dear

As I read your letter, I reflected on the fact that we have different understandings of the significance of the bachelor of science degree, though we certainly share common goals for the College. And even though I am sure that I cannot answer all of your concerns and observations, I would like to respond to just a few of them.

First of all, the administration was not involved with this decision. This was a decision made entirely by the faculty of the College, and the Board of Trustees acted only upon the recommendation of the faculty.

Secondly, our commitments to liberal arts have not diminished at all as a result of our offering the bachelor of science program. In fact, it is the conviction that persons working in the sciences should have a strong liberal arts education that has been the motivating factor behind Hope College's program for many years. We need well-educated, clear-thinking persons giving leadership in science, industry, government, as well as in the church.

Rather, the decision to offer the bachelor of science degree was primarily to designate more accurately the nature of the degree which these students have been completing for many years at Hope College. Our commitment to the liberal arts is not decreased at all by this decision. In fact, what concerns me the most is to force science majors, and also music majors, to take their undergraduate work in a college or university that does not have a strong commitment to the liberal arts.

Sincerely yours,

Dear

On behalf of the entire Hope College community, and also personally, I extend to you our sincere sympathy in the tragic loss of Steven. What a great loss this is to our community! But Steven's death is a much greater loss to you, his parents and wife. I write to share our love and concern.

Many of us in the Hope community have thought of you this past weekend and remembered you in our prayers. I know you have received the encouragement and support of countless others as well.

I trust that you have found the support and encouragement and the love of your family and friends to be a great source of strength at this time. I also trust that the memories you have of Steven, who was such a very remarkable individual, will also be very meaningful to you at this time. I also know that you have a deep personal faith and that this, with its promise and assurance of the resurrection, is very meaningful to you at this time.

I am sure that many questions remain in your minds. Most of these, no doubt, are questions of "why?" Why did this happen to Steven and to those who lost their lives with him? I have found over the years that "why" questions are very difficult and usually impossible to answer. There simply is no way that we can ultimately answer these questions. But what we can do is leave our "why" questions in the hands of a God of unbounded love and grace, who has come to us through Jesus Christ and the cross and the resurrection and Pentecost, and always be assured of his unfailing love. Further, he is able to take what are truly great tragedies and turn them into something significant and profitable with eternal dimensions. Much of this we are not privileged to see in this life. And yet I trust that from time to time you may catch a glimpse of how God has overcome the great tragedy of this event to bring his great purposes of love and grace and peace to the world.

We assure you of our continued love and support.

Sincerely yours,

Dear

I have received your letter relative to our professor's book. Let me respond briefly.

1. Is it legitimate, proper, and even necessary to evaluate significant religious trends in our denomination, the church and nation at large, and even the world? It seems to me that the answer to this question can only be affirmative, provided, of course, that such evaluation is done in love, fidelity to truth, and without attack on persons.

2. Is it legitimate and proper for a professor at one of the colleges affiliated with the RCA or one of the denominational seminaries to do such an evaluation? I believe it is. I would find it difficult, in fact impossible, to suggest to a faculty member that he or she not publish such an evaluation that he or she deems important. I believe that academic freedom calls for such freedom for a faculty member. At Hope, our emphasis on love, fairness, and grace would, of course, be particularly important, and I would have no reservation in stressing this.

   It would be particularly unfortunate if the criterion for advising someone not to speak or publish his or her convictions was the impact on financial contributions, even though none of us would deny the vital importance of such contributions to the College.

3. Does the book in question reflect the love, fidelity to truth, and grace that should mark a Christian's writing, particularly when writing about one's own denomination? This is, in my judgment, a very legitimate question. Whether the author has met this standard can only be judged when the book is published. I do know that the author has been unstinting in his commitment to achieve these high standards in writing, and to address only basic issues.

                                                    Sincerely yours,

Dear

I am writing in response to the letter I received about the article that appeared in the *Hope College News* about the Rev. A. J. Muste, who graduated from Hope College in 1905.

Rev. Muste was a Hope College graduate who had a distinguished record at Hope and became an ordained minister in the Reformed Church in America. He became a very well-known spokesman for the peace movement over a number of decades. While Hope College has never taken any official position relative to the peace movement, and the great majority of those associated with Hope would not identify with it, we do recognize that it is a point of view that we cannot totally ignore. Most of us at Hope believe that we as Christians should work harder for peace, though for most of us this will not take the pattern of activities that A. J. Muste engaged in. However, it was felt that we should take note of the 100th anniversary of the birth of a Hope graduate who was very well known. (The article printed was the opinion of one professor at Hope College and this was clearly identified as an article by this professor.)

There are two additional observations I would make. Just recently I had lunch with a friend of the College and we had a very pleasant discussion on this matter and other matters. While we do disagree on certain matters, we were able to have a very good time of fellowship together. I believe keenly that we must be able to maintain a genuine fellowship even when we disagree on certain matters. I believe that this is what our Lord and many Scriptures call us to do.

The other observation relates to the sentence that some allegations about the College "require your response." Over the years I have become convinced that not every allegation requires a response. I believe that our Lord recognized this, for, as we all know, he did not respond to every allegation. There is a tone in that statement which disturbs me a bit. It seems to me that it would be better to *invite* a response to such an allegation, rather than to *require* it. It is in such a spirit that we can keep the dialogue open, be ready to listen to each other, and thereby build up the body of Christ and maintain a deep sense of fellowship and mutual support, even when we may disagree on certain matters.

Sincerely yours,

The Honorable Guy Vander Jagt
United States House of Representatives
2409 Rayburn House Office Building
Washington, D.C. 20515

Dear Guy:

I have written to you and spoken to you on several occasions about
the new tax plan that you and your colleagues on the House Ways
and Means Committee will begin working on very intensively in the
near future. I truly appreciate your willingness to listen to our concerns, your sensitivity to these issues, and your consistent support for
the independent sector and for our emphasis on the best in quality and
values.

However, in view of the fact that you will be giving this matter
very diligent attention in the near future, I would like to share three
major concerns with you, and ask you to support positions on these
issues that are of vital importance to Hope College and all independent colleges.

1. Retain Tax-exempt Bonds for Independent Colleges.

For reasons I simply cannot comprehend, the administration tax
plan would eliminate the use of of tax-exempt bonds by independent colleges while retaining these for public institutions. Given
the strategic role that independent colleges play in providing quality education while saving tax dollars, this does not seem either
wise or equitable. I can testify that for Hope tax-exempt bonds
have been, and will continue to be, of vital importance. We used
tax-exempt bonds to finance the renovation of Voorhees Hall and
Durfee Hall and to construct the College East Apartments. We will
use tax-exempt bonds for interim financing for the construction of
the new library, which will be of great help to us in this important
undertaking. These tax-exempt bonds for the library are part of the
tax-exempt bond issue issued by the Michigan Higher Education
Facilities Authority that will benefit fifteen independent colleges
in Michigan.

Thus, tax-exempt bonds have made a vital difference at Hope
and have helped us achieve our commitment to excellence while

retaining the lowest possible cost to our students and their families. I hope you will be able to lend your support to the retention of tax-exempt bonds for construction of facilities at independent colleges, and, if possible, also for student loans.

2. Retain Full Deductibility of Appreciated Gifts.

Appreciated gifts continue to be of vital importance to Hope, as is true of all colleges and universities. This is especially significant in our current capital campaign. The fact that these gifts are fully deductible for tax purposes is an important incentive for making a larger gift than the donor would otherwise consider.

I realize that there has been some abuse of this provision, primarily because inflated values of such gifts have been reported. I heartily support every effort to eliminate abuse, as has been done in recent legislation. But I strongly urge that the full deductibility of appreciated gifts be retained. While charitable intent in making such gifts is always necessary, the full deductibility is a vital factor in the size of such gifts.

3. Retain the Non-itemizer Deduction for Charitable Contributions.

As you know, Hope does very well in receiving relatively small contributions from alumni, parents, and friends. Last year forty-three percent of our alumni contributed. In this case, also, a charitable intention is clearly the first step in making a gift. However, by retaining the non-itemizer deduction, the size of these gifts can be significantly increased. This is of vital importance to every charitable organization and particularly true for us at Hope College. This, too, is a provision that I hope you will be able to support.

I recognize the importance of tax reform, and I support many of the features in President Reagan's tax proposal. I do sincerely hope, however, that you will be able to support the three points that I have listed above. These will certainly help maintain the vitality of independent colleges and reduce the tax burden on government and taxpayers. I know that this also is of great concern to you.

If you have any questions or would like any specific data, please do not hesitate to contact me. Thank you very much for your willingness to listen to these concerns.

                                        Sincerely yours,

Dr. Gary R. Sullenger
Senate Fiscal Agency
P.O. Box 30036
Lansing, Michigan 48909

Dear Dr. Sullenger:

On behalf of Hope College, I express our appreciation for this opportunity to comment on the draft report from the Senate Select Committee on Higher Education.

Overall, I found this to be a very thoughtful, perceptive report. The most important issues raised by the Governor's Commission on the Future of Higher Education in Michigan were clearly identified and carefully addressed by the Senate Select Committee.

However, in regard to independent colleges, I take strong exception to the concept that these institutions "fill in the gaps left by the public higher education systems." The quality of the programs that some of the independent colleges have achieved, sometimes in direct competition with public institutions, should be taken into account. I would cite my own institution—Hope College—as an example. While the University of Michigan graduates the largest number of chemistry majors at the Baccalaureate level in the State, Hope College and Michigan State are tied for second in these numbers. In physics, Hope College is only slightly behind the University of Michigan in terms of the number of majors graduated. This record has been achieved because of the major emphasis we have on having undergraduates participate in research—something that large universities simply are not doing. Our science graduates have achieved remarkable records in both graduate and professional schools and compete with the best graduates of public institutions.

Many of the independent colleges in Michigan make distinctive contributions in other areas—some in the enrollment of minority students, some in the education of adults, some in serving inner-city students, some in being responsive to community needs.

Taken together, these institutions make a remarkable contribution to the programs and opportunities available to students in Michigan for higher education. In most cases, these are programs of outstanding quality. The records of these institutions speak for themselves.

Higher education students in Michigan deserve the opportunity for freedom of access and freedom of choice in attending the institution that best meets their needs. The state's financial investments in students in independent institutions is far less than in students in public institutions. Thus, independent institutions are truly a bargain for the state. Moreover, these institutions provide diversity, strength, and excellence to the higher education systems in Michigan.

The logical implication of the view that independent colleges and universities are "filling the gap" is that if the "gaps" were filled by public institutions, there would be no need for independent colleges. I believe it is far better to view independent institutions as offering a rich diversity in our higher education system through the way in which they blend, in a variety of ways, a commitment to excellence in teaching and scholarship, service to their local communities, emphasis on values, a personal dimension in education, and responsiveness to the needs of students and our citizens—all at a bargain for the taxpayer. This is the central reason why, in my judgment, the state should consider not only continuing, but increasing, support for students attending independent institutions in the State of Michigan.

Thank you for this opportunity to comment on this fine report by the Senate Select Committee.

Sincerely yours,

Autobiographical Sketch

GORDON J. VAN WYLEN

This autobiographical sketch was written at the suggestion of Dr. Boonstra and Dean Bruins, who thought it an appropriate way to provide insight into the author of these essays. Because of my esteem for these colleagues and my deep appreciation for their efforts in producing this volume, I was eager to comply.

I did not, however, find this an easy assignment. It was difficult to decide on the most important events of my pilgrimage and to determine what should be written and what should remain private. Further, while there are many memories of wonderful relationships with family, friends, and colleagues, there were also mistakes, distorted priorities, and failures in relationships and accomplishments. However, one of the results of grace is the ability to put these behind, to recall God's good gifts with gratitude, and to press forward to what lies ahead. It is from this perspective that I have written.

I was born in the rural area east of Grant, Michigan, to John and Effa Bierema Van Wylen. My parents moved to Grand Rapids when I was two years old. Our family included my older sister Margaret and my younger siblings Carol and Wayne.

Like so many of the children I grew up with, I was a second generation American of Dutch descent. My father was four years old when his family came to the United States. The family lived near Zeeland for a few years, where my grandfather worked in a brick factory, before moving to a farm near Grant, Michigan. A few years later, my grandfather died, leaving my grandmother with seven children. My father came to Grand Rapids as a young man to learn the carpentry trade. I recall that my father went to night school to learn drafting so that he could design homes, which was a key factor in enabling him later to have a small building firm of his own. I spent five summers during high school and college working for my father, from whom I learned much both in terms of skills and how to get things done, sometimes in adversity.

My mother, Effa Bierema, was born in Grand Rapids of parents who had emigrated from Friesland in the Netherlands a few years earlier. After living in Grand Rapids for some years, her family moved to a farm in Grant, where in due time my parents met. Though her formal education was limited, my mother was an avid reader, and even when her children were in college, she could discuss with them books she had read. It was from her that I first learned the joy of reading.

In my early years, family, church, and school were the focal points of the life of our family. Most of the holidays were spent visiting family members in Grant, and during the summer I often spent a few weeks with relatives, which enabled me to learn a bit about life on a farm. The family attended Oakdale Park Christian Reformed Church, and I recall that in my formative years I heard excellent preaching. I attended Oakdale Christian School from kindergarten through the ninth grade. Almost without exception, the teachers were superb, and even now I look back at these years as an excellent learning experience in content, in developing a love for learning, and in nurturing the Christian faith.

The Great Depression of the 1930s was a formative experience during my junior high and high school years. The building business eventually came to a complete halt, and though my father hung on as long as he could, eventually the family needed some government assistance. Even now I recall how the family resisted the step and how grateful they were when my father began his own business in 1935, with a contract to design and build a new home for a family.

It was because of the depression that on completing the ninth grade at Oakdale Christian School, I attended Ottawa Hills High

School rather than the Christian high school along with most of my classmates. Ottawa Hills High School had an outstanding faculty and students from quite diverse backgrounds—some affluent, some minorities, and many with limited income. In retrospect, this was a very significant step, for it enabled me to know and relate to a wide spectrum of people outside the rather structured environment I had experienced earlier. I feel now that the balance of solid Christian training in my early years, the experiences at Ottawa Hills, and the strong academic emphasis throughout were important gifts God provided in my early years.

On graduating from high school in 1937, the choices were quite limited and I decided to attend Calvin College, which was walking distance from home. With the memories of the depression fresh in mind, and with no great visions of a noble calling or an academic career, I decided to study engineering, a field which would provide a reasonable living. I decided to study pre-engineering at Calvin for three years and then transfer to the Engineering College at the University of Michigan. Enrollment at Calvin at that time was less than 500. Classes were small, the teachers excellent, and I developed many fine friendships. On completing my studies in 1940, I received the Rinck Prize in Mathematics, a recognition that carried the stipend of $20.00—a fairly significant sum in those years.

That fall I enrolled at the University of Michigan for my study of mechanical engineering, and I began an association with the university which would be far longer and significant than I could imagine at that time. Soon after arriving on campus, I became acquainted with Michigan Christian Fellowship, the local chapter of Inter-Varsity Christian Fellowship. This proved to be a very significant association, for I discovered in Inter-Varsity a group that took the university and scholarship seriously, while also stressing the importance of a genuine commitment to Jesus Christ and the development of Christian thought and practice, with an emphasis on gracious, sensitive Christian witness. I resonated with this approach and over the years this organization has been a vital part of my life.

Overall, the associations and experiences at Michigan were very rewarding. During my senior year, I served as a grader for two professors, which provided insights into academic work and initiated stirrings of exploring the possibility of an academic career for myself. I was elected to Tau Beta Pi, an engineering honor society, and in my senior year was awarded a Cornelius Donavan scholarship.

The Japanese attack on Pearl Harbor took place in December of my senior year, and suddenly everything, including prospects of a career in engineering, was dominated by a concern for World War II. Shortly before graduation I took a position as an engineer with the DuPont Company, in an inorganic chemical plant near Linden, New Jersey. Though it was a very fine experience to become familiar with the East Coast, I soon discovered that this was not the position to which I really aspired. Although the job did carry deferment from military service, I decided to join the V-7 program of the U.S. Navy. In February 1943, I began a four-month midshipman program on the old battleship *Prairie State*. The *Prairie State* was mired in the mud of the Hudson River at 137th Street. Though these were crowded quarters in which to live and study and the regimen of military service not particularly creative, I made many fine friendships, and in retrospect view my time on the *Prairie State* as a worthwhile experience.

There was no choice of assignments for graduating midshipmen, except that they could volunteer for submarine duty. Because I wanted to go to sea, rather than attend more navy schools, I volunteered for submarine duty and was assigned to the USS *Hardhead*, which was being built in Manitowoc, Wisconsin. After a shakedown period in Lake Michigan, the *Hardhead* traveled to the Chicago area, where it was lifted out of the water in a floating drydock and pushed down the Mississippi River to

New Orleans by a large tugboat. This very delightful trip in the spring of 1944 provided a vivid background to reading Mark Twain's *Life on the Mississippi.* On leaving New Orleans, the *Hardhead* passed through the Panama Canal and on to Pearl Harbor. From there we left on our first war patrol on the east coast of the Philippines, and sixty-three days later arrived in Perth, West Australia, our permanent base. The frequent visits to Australia were very fine experiences, and I particularly enjoyed my associations with the Inter-Varsity Christian Fellowship group at the University of West Australia.

When the war ended, I had completed six war patrols on the *Hardhead* and the boat was in Subic Bay in the Philippines preparing for another patrol. These six patrols had been marked by a great deal of action, both attacking and being attacked, and I still recall the tremendous sense of relief which came when the war was over. At that time, the full impact of the atomic bomb was not known, but I recall very vividly feeling that this did end all the bloodshed and strife of the past six years, and gave a welcome end to the war.

Yet, even in these years I learned much that helped me in later life. Serving as an officer on a submarine provided remarkable opportunities for assuming major responsibilities, making decisions, often without much time for reflection, living with frequent exposure to dangers and the possibility of death, and dealing with a diverse group of people in a crowded and less-than-desirable environment. Frequently there was time to read, and on one patrol I completed *War and Peace,* a truly remarkable environment in which to read this classic. This was also a time of significant spiritual growth, and I frequently led a church service in the ship's dining room for those who were interested. Years later, when I stood outside a burning Van Raalte Hall in April 1980, the memories of some difficult moments during the war flooded my mind and the same confidence in God provided stability and courage.

It was also during this period that I decided to pursue a career in teaching engineering. When discharged from the navy in February 1946, I enrolled immediately in a master's degree program at the University of Michigan, and continued through that summer.

There were two significant events during this period. The first was receiving an appointment as instructor in mechanical engineering at Pennsylvania State University, beginning in the fall of 1946, which enabled me to begin an academic career and to see if this was indeed my calling. The second was meeting Margaret DeWitt, a freshman medical student, in an Inter-Varsity group, during the summer of 1946. Margaret had graduated from Duke University in 1945 with plans to be a medical missionary. Late in the summer of 1945 she deferred her enrollment in medical school for one year, in order to have a year of biblical and theological study at Biblical Seminary in New York.

The romance was slow in maturing—one date at the end of that summer. With my going off to Pennsylvania State University at the end of the summer school, and Margaret beginning her freshman year in medical school, we realized that though we were attracted to each other, neither was sure where the relationship might go. But the second date did come off—nine months later during our spring vacation in 1947.

I taught at Pennsylvania State University for two years, from 1946 to 1948, and completed my master's degree at Michigan during the summer of 1947. My favorite subject was thermodynamics and I became convinced that I should make a career of teaching this subject. So during the spring of 1948 I made arrangements to enroll in a doctoral program at Massachusetts Institute of Technology (MIT). Since this program involved passing examinations in both French and German, I studied French during my last year at Pennsylvania. But a much more exciting plan evolved for studying German. My friend, Brevard Childs, who later became a distinguished professor of Old Testament at Yale Theological School, and I spent the summer of 1948 traveling in Europe and studying German at the University of Zurich. While in Europe we had the opportunity to attend a meeting of the International Fellowship of Evangelical Students, which proved to be a very significant spiritual experience. And during this entire period Margaret and I continued to write to each other and see each other during each vacation in the academic year. Gradually, we sensed that God was drawing us together, but our sense of God's calling for our individual lives seemed so divergent.

I began my graduate studies at MIT in the fall of 1948 with a fairly high degree of confidence, since I had always been a good student. Soon, however, I realized that this was a very different environment. The demands of the faculty were very high and the caliber of the students far higher than I had ever experienced before. So the first semester was very difficult, and on more than one occasion, I wondered if I was on the right track. But as I thought and prayed about this matter, God seemed to confirm that an academic career was my calling. By the end of the first semester I had made the adjustment to the MIT expectations and environment and began to enjoy my studies, the friendships I made, and attending Park Street Church and hearing Dr. Harold Ockinga preach. Through my involvement with Inter-Varsity at MIT, I gained many wonderful friends, including Kenneth Olsen, an outstanding undergraduate student who later became the founder of Digital Equipment Corporation.

During the 1948 academic year Margaret and I wrote regularly to each other and we began to study the same passages of the Bible in our daily readings and shared our thoughts and insights with each other. We also saw each other a great deal during our vacation periods, and when Margaret came east during the summer of 1949 (ostensibly to visit her sister who lived in Providence!), we found many opportunities to see each other, and before the summer was over we were engaged and planning to be married the following June. For our careers, we saw the opportunity to serve abroad, perhaps in a developing country, with Margaret in medicine and me in engineering education. Margaret received an internship at Mount Auburn Hospital in Cambridge, and I rented an apartment nearby. By spring vacation Margaret had purchased her wedding dress and made final plans for the wedding.

Just before leaving the Boston area to spend the vacation in Michigan, I learned that Margaret was a patient in the Student Health Service at Michigan with a bad cold. On arriving in Ann Arbor I went immediately to see her, but before being allowed to do so, I was informed by the doctor that Margaret had contracted tuberculosis and would be a patient in University Hospital for some time. Suddenly all our plans were changed, both immediate and long range. We both recall very vividly how our prayers for guidance and our experience of God's love and grace in Jesus Christ sustained us as we made this difficult adjustment.

That spring vacation ended with Margaret in complete bed rest at University Hospital and my returning to MIT to continue my thesis research. It was difficult to make any plans because of the uncertainty of how long the cure would take, and what would be appropriate thereafter in careers and service. Margaret and I continued our joint study of the Bible, and even began playing chess by mail. I attributed Margaret's regular wins in chess to having more time to consider each move, but deep down knew it was simply a matter of her being a better chess player!

Gradually, new plans emerged. I saw the possibility of completing my thesis by January 1951, and accepted a position as assistant professor at the University of Michigan. Margaret and I were now able to visit regularly in the hospital and to celebrate together when, after eleven months of complete bed rest, Margaret could sit on the edge of the bed for five minutes a day. Gradually her activities began to increase, and in August, when she had two and one-half hours a day out of bed, she was discharged, sixteen months after entering the hospital. We then made plans to be married in December, and when this event finally arrived, Margaret had five hours a day out of bed. My father had designed and begun building a new home for us in Ann Arbor, which we moved into after a few months of apartment living while the house was being finished.

When I began my work at Michigan, I soon became immersed in teaching thermodynamics to undergraduates and graduates and supervising doctoral students in their research. While at MIT I had studied thermodynamics under Professor Joseph Keenan, a brilliant professor who was very rigorous in his treatment of the subject. His textbook was a standard work, but difficult to read. When I began teaching, I found no textbook that seemed to combine the rigor of Professor Keenan with the readability needed for undergraduates. So I began preparing notes to supplement the textbooks I used, and in my writing I tried to find this balance between rigor and clarity. By 1954 I had accumulated a fairly large amount of material, and I began to think about the possibility of writing a thermodynamics textbook. A number of publishers were interested, and in 1955 I signed a contract with John Wiley & Sons. There followed a demanding three-year period in which I devoted almost all of my spare time to preparing this textbook. Upon publication it gained wide acceptance almost immediately and soon captured most of the market from a dozen or so competing books; its various editions have been translated into French, Portuguese, Spanish, Hindi, and Arabic.

One aspect of thermodynamics that has always intrigued me was the second law of thermodynamics, for it has definite implications for such issues as the direction of time, the origin of the universe, and the concept that natural processes proceed in directions so that a system and its surroundings can never return to their original state. This is often expressed as the principle of the increase of entropy. This principle has significant theological implications, and I included a carefully worded statement on this matter in the textbook, which reads as follows:

> The author has found that the second law tends to increase his conviction that there is a Creator who has the answer to the future destiny of man and the universe.

Many students were surprised to find such a statement in a textbook, and I have received comments from many persons that this simple statement was of help to them as they thought about the Christian faith during their college years.

After our marriage, Margaret and I agreed that Margaret should complete the two months of medical school that she lacked for completing her medical degree. She did this on a half-time basis and graduated with the class of 1952. We also agreed that with the recovery from tuberculosis still in process, she should not undertake the rigors of an internship and that this was an appropriate time to begin a family. Before doing so, however, Margaret did some teaching in the anatomy department of the University of Michigan Medical School.

Our first child, Elizabeth, was born in 1953, followed by Stephen in 1955, Ruth in 1957, David in 1958, and Emily in 1964. These were very busy days for Margaret, as well as for me, as I was busy at the university and with my writing and research. In 1956 I accepted an invitation to serve on the Board of Trustees of Inter-Varsity Christian Fellowship, and a few years later was elected chairman of the board. Shortly after I was elected, the president, C. Stacy Woods, who had led Inter-Varsity in the United States since its founding in 1940, resigned, which gave me the added responsibility of leading the process to select a successor. Taking these responsibilities also proved to be fortuitous, for I learned a good deal about organization, management, and the role of the Board of Trustees—information that would be of great help to me when I assumed the presidency of Hope.

The decade of the 1950s was significant in three other respects. For several years Margaret and I were uncertain as to what church we should join in Ann Arbor. Margaret was still a member of First Presbyterian Church in Grand Haven and I was a member of Park Street Church in Boston. In 1955 we decided to cast our lot with a newly organized Christian Reformed Church. The goal of the church was to develop into a congregation that would minister and reach out to persons of different backgrounds and cultures, and be much more heterogeneous than the traditional Christian Reformed Church. Over the years this was achieved in significant measure, and our associations with the church proved to be a source of blessing and led to many lasting friendships.

A second important activity involved international students at the university. Since Margaret and I were not able to go abroad, we decided to make a special effort to entertain foreign students in our home. From this evolved a Saturday evening Bible study and social time that was attended by many international students over the years. One result was the help we gave to a number of these students as they planned their weddings, and on half a dozen occasions I gave the bride away. A number of these students became Christians and later took active roles in their churches in this country or in their home countries. This also provided a wonderful opportunity for our children to be friends with people from many different places and cultures.

The third event of this period was my first appointment to an administrative position, when, in 1958, I accepted the invitation to serve as chairman of the Department of Mechanical Engineering. This department had about 35 faculty members, 400 undergraduates, and 100 graduate students, and the chairmanship required at least half of my time. I continued to teach one course and supervise the work of graduate students. One important aspect of both my research and administrative responsibilities was to secure external funding, which involved writing grant proposals and encouraging others to do the same. This experience proved to be very valuable to me in later years in fund-raising at Hope College.

The decade of the 1960s was marked primarily by a continuation of activities begun earlier. Emily, our fifth child, was born in 1964. In 1965 I was appointed dean of the College of Engineering, which was a full-time responsibility and involved me in many university-wide concerns, and provided the opportunity to lead one of the nation's premier engineering colleges. At that time, there were 3,000 undergraduates and 1,000 graduate students in the College of Engineering. Little did I realize when I took this position that the student protest movement of the late 1960s would have a significant impact on the College of Engineering, and that this would call for leadership of a different kind than I had been involved in before. I served as dean until 1972, when I was appointed president of Hope College, and I look at these years as a time of great personal growth and a wonderful opportunity to learn the responsibilities of leadership, management, and administration.

The home that my father had built in 1951 was proving to be too small, and in the late 1960s we began planning a new home, which we anticipated would be suitable for the rest of our lives. We picked out a lot in a newly developed area where we had often gone for walks over the years, and my father developed a very attractive design for the home. Little did we realize, when we moved into this home in the spring of 1970, that in just over two years we would move into a lovely ninety-year-old home on the Hope College campus.

From time to time I had been invited to explore the possibility of becoming a candidate for president of a college or university, and on a few occasions had proceeded as far as a preliminary discussion. In the fall of 1971 Hope College and another university invited me to explore the possibility of serving as president. I remember a very helpful conversation with Roger Heyns, a friend since Calvin College days, who had served as vice president for Academic Affairs at the University of Michigan before undertaking the very challenging assignment in the mid-1960s of serving as chancellor of the University of California at Berkeley. Heyns was in Ann Arbor in the fall of 1971, and I asked his advice on these possibilities, though I was secretly hoping Roger's advice would be to stay in Ann Arbor. The counsel Roger gave made a great impression, and I have often passed this on to others. Roger's advice was, "It is a great thing to have a new challenge in one's late forties or early fifties. I would seriously think about taking one of these positions if offered. And of the two, I would think most about Hope College."

The decision to invite me to become president must have been, in many ways, a difficult one for Hope College. In my latter years at Hope I could quip that, in relation to Hope College, I was from the wrong profession (engineering), the wrong undergraduate college (Calvin), the wrong denomination (Christian Reformed), and the wrong institution (a large state university) to serve as president of an undergraduate liberal arts college affiliated with the Reformed Church in America. When the invitation was extended, it was very difficult for our family to decide to leave our home, schools, church, and friends, as well as the security and opportunities at the University of Michigan, to take the position as president, particularly at a time when college presidents were having very difficult experiences. Coupled with this was all the uncertainty of not knowing whether this was a position I could handle. In the final days of making the decision, it was the opportunity to be associated with a distinguished Christian liberal arts college and the sense that this was God's call that tipped the balance.

In retrospect, the years at Hope were very rewarding for me personally and for us as a family. One of the unexpected benefits for Margaret was the opportunity to return to medicine. Shortly after arriving in Holland we met Donald Walchenbach, a Hope alumnus who at that time headed Butterworth Hospital in Grand Rapids. Walchenbach assured Margaret that she could do an in-

ternship on a part-time basis. Margaret's commitment was to put
her family and the College ahead of her career, so she took four
and one-half years to complete a one-year internship. This pace
gave her time to get back into medicine after a lapse of more than
twenty years. On completing this internship, she did a residency
in psychiatry at Michigan State University and Pine Rest Christian Hospital, again primarily on a part-time basis. On completing this, she practiced psychiatry, almost always on a part-time
basis, at Ottawa County Mental Health Department, Holland
Community Hospital, and Child and Family Services. Her Christian commitment, her experiences as a wife and mother of five
children, and her natural love for people enabled her to serve her
clients with courage, sensitivity, and compassion.

As I wrote this autobiographical sketch and reflected on my
years at Hope, three things stood out in my mind. The first is the
great privilege it was to be associated for fifteen years with so
many wonderful people—trustees, faculty members, staff members, students, alumni, and friends of the college. Working with
these wonderful colleagues and friends provided joys beyond
telling and was a most rewarding experience.

The second is the countless ways in which I sensed God's
guidance and grace during the years. What a freeing experience it
is, after we have done our best, to leave matters in God's hands
and to know that often he does far more than we could ask or
think.

Finally, though the idea of serving as a college president
scarcely entered my mind during the first five decades of my life,
it is remarkable how a host of diverse experiences helped prepare
me for these responsibilities. Such are the ways in which God in
his goodness leads us.

I am grateful to God for his faithfulness, and to Margaret, my
family, and many colleagues and friends for their love, encouragement, and support along the way.